THE SPIRIT OF SANITY

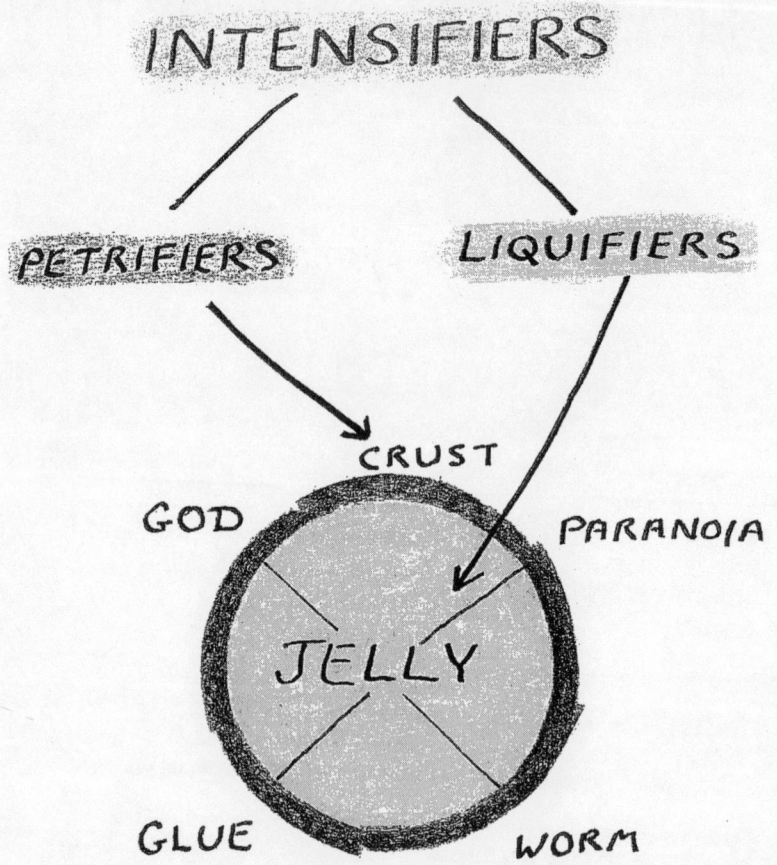

THE SPIRIT OF SANITY

Neville Symington

LONDON   NEW YORK

First published in 2001 by
H. Karnac (Books) Ltd.
6 Pembroke Buildings, London NW10 6RE

A subsidiary of Other Press LLC, New York

Copyright © 2001 Neville Symington

Reprinted 2002

The rights of Neville Symington to be identified as the author of this work have been asserted in accordance with §§ 77 and 78 of the Copyright Design and Patents Act 1988.

All rights reserved. No part of this publication may be reproduced, stored in a retrieval system, or transmitted, in any form or by any means, electronic, mechanical, photocopying, recording, or otherwise, without the prior written permission of the publisher.

British Library Cataloguing in Publication Data

A C.I.P. for this book is available from the British Library

ISBN 1 85575 265 4

10 9 8 7 6 5 4 3 2 1

www.karnacbooks.com

Printed and bound in Great Britain by Biddles Ltd, *www.biddles.co.uk*

*This book is dedicated to
Joan Smith
whose selfless love over 60 years
is responsible for much of the inspiration in these pages*

CONTENTS

PREFACE ix

INTRODUCTORY REMARKS
Isca Wittenberg 1

MEDITATION ONE
An ontology for sanity 3

MEDITATION TWO
Freedom and survival 25

MEDITATION THREE
A pattern of madness 41

MEDITATION FOUR
Emotional action and strengthening of the ego 61

MEDITATION FIVE
God and the worm 77

MEDITATION SIX
Trauma and attachment — 103

MEDITATION SEVEN
How our technique is affected by this outlook — 117

MEDITATION EIGHT
The spirit of sanity: discussion of central issues — 129

CLOSING REMARKS
Isca Wittenberg — 149

APPENDIX A
The true god and the false god — 153

APPENDIX B
An exegesis of conscience in the works of Freud — 167

APPENDIX C
Envy: a psychological analysis — 183

APPENDIX D
"I feel a fraud" — 192

REFERENCES — 203

PREFACE

This book is the outcome of a conference that took place at the Tavistock Clinic from the 19th to the 21st of September 1999. It came about in this way: I had been writing a book, *The Pattern of Madness,* and I had been discussing aspects of it with Cesare Sacerdoti of Karnac Books and also with Isca Wittenberg, who had been a Senior Child Psychotherapist for many years at the Tavistock. Both of them thought that a lecture from me on the subject of the book would be welcome when I was next in England. This presented me with a problem. I knew that it was not possible to convey the theory and practice I was trying to develop in one lecture and therefore said that I would be willing to offer a series of talks. Thus it came about that I gave seven lectures at this conference, and there was an eighth session devoted entirely to discussion. The lectures and discussion were taped and transcribed, and the text of this book is an edited version of both the lectures and discussion. I have deliberately left the spoken style of the conference intact. What is lost in literary style is gained in immediacy of exposition. I have only removed things like "ums" "ahs" and "sort ofs" and bits of text that referred to practical aspects of the conference, like the time of the next lecture and so on. I have left the questions from the floor as they were presented. I have only cut out those questions that had already been asked and were therefore passed over. I have added to my answers some sentences to clarify and add precision where I have thought necessary.

Madness consists of a series of elements that interconnect to make up a pattern. This pattern can only be seen against the backdrop of a schema that delineates sanity. The fact that my model of sanity is conceptualized according to a religious philosophical outlook will deter some people. I would emphasize, however, that I define "religious" as encompassing two dimensions: (1) freedom of choice and, (2) the mind's inability to grasp conceptually certain existential paradoxes. These are the two pillars upon which are built the elaborate frameworks which we encounter in the great religions of mankind. It is out of this kernel that I build my theory of sanity, and it is against that backdrop that madness is silhouetted.

I have too many people to thank, so I limit myself just to Isca Wittenberg and Cesare Sacerdoti, who had the inspiration and confidence to plan this conference.

THE SPIRIT OF SANITY

Introductory remarks

Isca Wittenberg

It gives me enormous pleasure to welcome Neville back here to the Tavistock, because as you will have seen from the programme he was in fact a member of the Adult Department of the Tavistock of 1977–85, and during that time students were enormously stimulated by the lectures that he gave, which eventually were published in book form as *The Analytic Experience*, which I think is a most wonderful introduction to what psychoanalysis and the psychoanalytic experience is like. Neville has gone on to publish a number of other books which will be displayed tomorrow and on Sunday, and each one is full of most original thought which is enormously stimulating and challenging, and full of courage to face issues which most of us don't.

I think that this is a very special conference, to which I have been looking forward enormously for quite some time. The theme, of course, is an unusual one to have in a psychoanalytic institution like the Tavistock: the spirit, the spiritual dimension of sanity in mental health and in psychoanalysis. When I first came here I was interviewed by a psychiatrist/psychoanalyst Dr Hunter—in fact, the father-in-law of Jonathan Bradley, and the father of someone who then became a child psychotherapist—and when he heard that my father had been a rabbi and I had been brought up in a rabbinical household, he said, "Well, I suppose psychotherapy is the modern priesthood." When I studied psychoanalysis here, it didn't quite seem like that. It seemed much more that the tradition of Freud was rather hostile to religion and the religious outlook; it was seen as something rather ill, neurotic and illusory, and, of course, it involved a personal struggle for me. How could I take up this work and think about the spiritual dimension? So, of course, this is what attracted me particularly to Neville's book *Emotion and Spirit*, in which he tackles, in a very new, original way, what is a religious philosophy that does fit in with psychoanalysis.

This is also a very special conference, because it is most unusual to have just one speaker for a whole weekend. In fact, I can only remember it happening when Dr Bion was here. Usually there are many speakers and many different presenters and discussions. I think that this gives us the opportunity to listen to Neville, for him to develop his ideas, to tell us how they came about, and it gives us the opportunity to ask, to ask him, to ask ourselves, and to open our minds to new thought. It is my great hope that this will be a wonderful exchange between all of us and Neville, but also among all of ourselves as well on this enormously important subject, and that we will go away at the end of this weekend with new ideas and a deepening of understanding. I am sure that we will have a very good time together. Thank you.

MEDITATION ONE

An ontology for sanity

The first thing that I would like to do is to thank Isca, who was the one who hatched this conference. She hatched it in dialogue with Cesare Sacerdoti; they had some conversations together, and so they have been like good parents giving birth to a child. I would also like to thank them for another reason—or, perhaps, thank the Tavistock for another reason: they have put huge faith in me when they don't know what is going to come forth. I do think—and I refer to this in some of the talks—that a capacity to take an act of faith is one of the things that strengthens the personality. Another aspect of this that pleased me enormously was that they asked me for no abstract or summary of my talks in advance. I have been to many conferences over the years, and nearly always, about three or six months earlier, I have been asked for either the paper or an abstract, and this is a method of killing a conference. What I say today won't be quite the same as I would have said three months ago. We develop all the time, and this has been true for me now. In the last few days I have been staying near to the National Gallery and have gone and looked at some paintings, and I got quite an understanding from looking at one of the paintings, which will come up in one of the lectures. If I had had to produce all the material for the conference six months ago, then this new insight would not have been present.

I am also grateful to the Tavistock for taking the faith to have me for the whole weekend. I do not know yet how it will turn out, but I do think that there is quite a virtue in trying to get a unity of theme, because it is my experience in many conferences that one hears one paper, then one hears another, then you hear another, and then you hear another, and in the end there is nothing but a confusion of tongues. I have a bee in my bonnet: that in modern culture, of which the psychotherapy and psychoanalytic worlds are a part, we do not internalize sufficiently; we don't take things in, in a deep way. For that reason, I have called these lectures "meditations", to emphasize the idea that through emotional meditation acts of understanding can occur. If, when I read a paper or go to a conference, I have one act of understanding that I did not have before, then I rate it a success. If any one of you here has one act of understanding that illuminates something that you hadn't quite realized before, I will feel that it has been satisfactory. So it is not a conference in which you are going to be loaded with a whole lot of facts. Think of it more as a musical composition in which there is one theme but many manifestations. I don't know whether any of you have read the philosopher Schopenhauer, but at the beginning of his book *The World As Will and Representation*, he says: "There is only one idea here"—and the book is about one thousand pages long, and therefore, I think, he quite wisely says—"When you have finished it if you want to understand it, you must re-read it." I know exactly what he means, because he has one idea, and the whole book is an attempt to manifest that idea. It is manifest through the different parts, but then you need to go through it all again in order to grasp it. I have in recent years taken a cue out of his recommendation, and I have found that any book really worth reading, I need to read twice—which also makes me always be rather careful what I read.

The other thing that I think is very important is that if any of us have an act of understanding where we suddenly understand something, or have a realization and something is illuminated, it means that we grasp the unity that there is in diversity, and it is quite a difficult idea to get hold of. I am hoping that in this first meditation it might be possible to get this across, because it is quite central, and, what is more, it also goes very much against the ethos of the age. Post-modern culture travels along the surface of things, linguistic philosophy places meaning in terms of where particular words are within the structure of a sentence, but what I am saying is that meaning is seeing the unity not separate from diversity, but within it. You can't separate it from the diversity. So, for instance, if you have a realization about someone—it might or might not be a patient—you suddenly realize, "My Heavens! This person is full of shame." It is not something that you can isolate as if it were just one little corner of the personality; you realize that it permeates all sorts of aspects of their personality.

We have spoken about a religious philosophy. When you talk about religion or a religious philosophy or you use words like "mystical", people immediately think of something that is waffly and muddle-headed. In fact, I think that it is the exact opposite. To think about what I call a religious philosophy requires one to meditate deeply and to think. As I said in my book on *Emotion and Spirit*, people tend to say that something is scientific as long as it is within the canons of a positivistic and determinist type of philosophy, and, of course, that is not a correct definition of science. That which is scientific is what corresponds most closely to the data of experience, to the way human beings think and behave. In my view, a religious philosophy fits best with the fact that human beings all act according to inner intentions and desires.

Many people will often say, "Oh well, as long as someone is a good clinician, a good practical clinician, it doesn't matter what theory they have, and if they've got a rather determinist positivistic theory, that doesn't matter", but I don't think that is correct, because the background actually affects the way you see the object. I'm just going to give you a little example here (see pp. 6, 7). Now, you see that? You see these elephants, and you see the Savannah grass, and you look at that, and I don't know what you think it might be—it might be a tiger, perhaps a leopard or something. And here is exactly the same object—exactly the same object, you see.

It's a slightly gimmicky sort of example, but, in fact, I put the problem to my wife who did all the visual aids, and she produced this, which I think best shows the idea that in fact the background way of thinking does illuminate the foreground.

I don't know if any of you have come across a book by John Macmurray. He is a philosopher/thinker who has influenced me a great deal. He tells the story of a young hunter in South Africa (Macmurray, 1936),who day after day went out from the camp but came home empty-handed. Then one day an old hunter went with him; they walked for a while, and then the old hunter suddenly stopped, and they both froze. The experienced hunter pointed to a wood, and the young one, the boy, said, "I can't see anything." The old one said, "Well, go on looking." After looking for another two minutes, the boy said excitedly, "Oh, yes, I see! There's an antelope in the trees", and the old hunter said, "Yes, you can see now because you know the pattern to look for." Some people who have heard me on this may think I am being over-pessimistic, but I think there is a crisis in the world of psychoanalysis and psychotherapy because we are looking at the wrong thing. It is a commonplace that we know many people who have been analysed, who have had therapy, but we refer to them as being very narcissistic, self-orientated, and self-centred. One reason for this is, I believe, that we have got our sights on the wrong thing. Say, for instance, you have someone who suffers from a very powerful sense of inferiority. What's the reason? You might say the reason is that he's never been validated properly by his parents; you may say he feels inferior because he is short in height, or he belongs to a nation that's

been conquered in war recently, or that he has received inadequate mothering. All these ideas flow from the idea that the inferiority is imprinted through what has been done to the person. Yet what I have noticed clinically is this: that if someone gives of himself with emotional generosity, his inferiority diminishes. If this is true, then it implies a very different picture. If I am looking for what has been done and not at what is being done, then I won't see the antelope in the trees. If, on the other hand, I notice the inner withdrawal, the inner meanness, then I am seeing something that is closely related to the feelings of inferiority. I am seeing the antelope. So my conclusion here is that part of what leads to inferiority is someone being unable or being blocked from inner acts of generosity and

love. These are attitudes of mind that are the ideal of all great religions; I have not seen the reason for a sense of inferiority being explained in this way in psychoanalytic literature—at least not explicitly. I will give you an example of what I mean. If you are making assumptions according to classical analytic thinking, and you meet someone who feels very inferior, or you have a patient who suffers from a strong sense of inferiority, and you have the feeling that it is because they haven't been understood properly or they have been put down by people, and so on, you will have missed that essential thing. You won't help the patient to remove those blocks that may enable him to make a free emotional act. I will come to the importance of freedom in the next meditation. Yet if what I am saying is correct, then a religious philosophy brings us right into the central drama of what causes inferiority.

Now, there is one other thing I just want to say. This is more of the background, and that's a question of language. I have been criticized a certain amount for using words like "virtue", "moral", and so on, and so there is a question as to whether it's best to dig out old language and reinvest it with its real meaning or to invent new language. "Virtue" comes from the Latin *virtus*, which means strength, and "moral" means a person's own inner acts guided by conscience. But most people tend to think that the word "virtue" is equivalent to "pietistic". Nearly everyone to whom I've used the word "moral" immediately thinks that you mean moralistic, but they are totally different things. "Moral" refers to a person's inner direction in terms of good or bad, whereas moralistic is my condemnatory judgement of another according to their external behaviour. So the question is whether or not you use these old words. My own view is it is better to use the old words and try and invest them with their proper meaning. One of the reasons for this is that if you do that, you find then that your discourse and your way of talking links you with people in other disciplines. So, for instance, if you use the word "moral", it links you with moral philosophers, with people writing on ethics, with theologians, and so on, and the word virtue does the same.

I also often hear people talking about projective identification or identification, or depression, or whatever, and then they say, "Ah, but I don't speak to my patients like that." Actually, I have come to suspect that that's not true: I think they actually do, and I have evidence that they do. Part of the problem is that language of that sort doesn't touch the heart, and part of the whole endeavour of psychotherapy and psychoanalysis is to touch and move the heart. I was in Israel recently, and while in Jerusalem, I read a book about King David. When I returned home I read the biblical account of King David, and there is a very nice little instance in it, though I don't think it's one of the very well known episodes. Before David had become king and conquered Jerusalem, he was in a particular area, and his soldiers were guarding the flocks of sheep that belonged to a rich man called Nabal. When the time for sheep-shearing arrived, which was also a time for celebration, David sent one of his soldiers to Nabal and said, "Listen, would you let us join in the festivities and give a bit of food and wine to us soldiers?" And Nabal said, "No, no" and "Who are you?" When the soldiers told David of Nabal's attitude, he was absolutely furious, and he said, "I am going to come down and slaughter the lot of them." However, Nabal's wife, Abigail, thought she'd try to do something about this, and so she went to David and took some gifts of goats and sheep and some cheese and some wine, and she said that her husband was a bit of a callous type of fellow and not to pay too much attention to him. So David accepted this gift. When Abigail got back and told Nabal what she had done, this is how the Bible puts it: "His heart died within him, and he became a stone." Is that not more expressive than saying, "he became very depressed"? In his essay on "Politics and the English Language", which is not so much about politics as about the English language, George Orwell says that it's mental laziness that makes us just go immediately for the first cliché that's on the shelf. He says that it takes an effort to use your imagination and find a way of expressing what you intend so that it's alive. I think this is tremendously important. I remember when I worked here at the Tavistock, I thought one day that if I heard the term "projective identification" once more, I'd jump out of a window! But, you see, even if you use a word like "identification", it's stripped of all meaning; but if you say instead, "I put my whole spirit into Ronald's mind", then that means something, and you can feel what is meant. You might think, "heavens, that's a rather stupid thing to do", or you might admire it, but you can't be neutral to such a statement. So, getting the right language is very important. It does relate to a religious philosophy, because the religious way of speaking is much more poetic and touches the heart more deeply. "I put my spirit into Ronald's way of thinking" is a religious metaphor. "I identified with Ronald" is anodyne language.

I also want to emphasize the need to siphon out what is central, what is best, from all the great religious traditions. By all the great religious traditions, I mean Judaism, Islam, Christianity, Hinduism, Buddhism, Janism, and Zoroastrianism. It's quite clear to me that all these religions have a great treasure inside them; unfortunately they are also all enfleshed in a lot of peripheral stuff, stuff that is not right, stuff that has served to obscure the central thing. It is clear that the world is in a precarious state and that there has been an appalling collapse of values. There's a need in all of us who have an attachment to particular religious affiliations to be prepared to look at what's really essential and what's good, and also to say, "Well, perhaps that's not quite so good." I think perhaps the Hindus have a better understanding here, or the Buddhists a better understanding there, and so on. Also, my conclusion is that there's no religion that doesn't have some deficit that could in fact be supplanted or sort of supplemented by a viewpoint from one of the other great religions.

* * *

This meditation is called "An Ontology for Sanity", and I shall try to explain what I mean by ontology. I shall start with the very ancient dilemma of the philosopher Parmenides. Parmenides, who lived before Socrates and therefore also before Aristotle and Plato, looked out on the world and saw that it was very varied and changeable, but when he reflected, when he closed his eyes and just reflected on the reality of what he had taken in through his senses, he said to himself, "Well, there is only one thing, one reality." And so he said, "Oh, so all the world of change and variety out there must be an illusion." Now obviously all of us know that that must be nonsense, but he wasn't a fool. He realized that if you reflect upon yourself, there is a oneness: that a table, human beings, the universe as a whole are one; that existence is one, it cannot be other than a unity. Socrates, Plato, and in particular Aristotle tried to solve that problem, but they weren't able to do so. Their answers are not satisfactory. But, you see, I think the central religious position is to recognize that there is a dilemma—that the human mind is limited and not able to grasp the answer to this paradox. Quite how the two fit together is beyond the capacity of the human mind to grasp, and this is what is meant in all the great religions by the word "mystery". I say that because often the word "mystery" is used in a completely vulgarized form to refer to something that is enigmatic or strange, but that is not the meaning of it. The seers who wrote and devised the Upanishads—this is the other difference between religion and philosophy—reached a deep contemplation of the world and its nature, of which they were a part. Because they realized that they were a part of the world, of the universe, it meant that their actual way of living was affected by what they understood. Their contemplative vision implies that human beings and the whole world is in itself infinite, absolute. I think that if it's possible to get hold of this idea, it is exceedingly illuminating because it affects our understanding of many psychological factors. I just might perhaps give an example, to which I'll come again later. For instance, people very often think that guilt refers to regret about damage done to another. I don't think, though, that that's the meaning of guilt, nor is it why conscience basically reproaches one. It means that you are doing something against the infinite or the absolute in which the other person and you participate, it's part of the nature of both and not only both, but of everyone. It seems to me exceedingly important to grasp that. I have had quite a number of discussions with people, for instance, about guilt, and I think it's always, always misunderstood. A guilty act is always self-damaging and damaging to the other person. That is just one example of how the infinite is relevant.

Let us look at where religious philosophy leads us. I just want to divide it very crudely, for a moment, into East and West. I think the Eastern philosophy—Hinduism and Buddhism—understood that the absolute is actually part of our being, part of our constitution, that is inseparable from us, and that through a contemplative act one can reach an understanding of it. To go back to what I said about these talks being meditations: meditation, in the way I understand it and the way I was brought up to understand it, is a sort of reflection in a deep way on one particular thing. It may be a particular person or a particular event or a particular theme, but the ultimate aim of all meditation is to arrive at contemplation, which is an intuitive act of understanding that goes beyond the surface sensory forms. That I think is the great contribution of the tradition that comes from Hinduism and Buddhism. But I think—and I'm talking here of essentials—the great contribution of Judaism, Christianity, and Islam was the realization that this absolute was personal. Therefore the whole drama in the history of God's covenant with the Israelites is a person-to-person situation.

How the infinite is one but varied is a mystery; how the infinite is personal is also a mystery. In other words, there is evidence through reflection that it is so; yet you can't ever completely grasp *how* it is possible. There are two ways in which spiritual people have tried to understand the dilemma. One way comes from Hinduism, but I think it was represented in the West by the philosopher Spinoza, who said everything is one substance. He called that substance God but emphasized that he did not mean by it the God as revealed in the Scriptures of Judaism and Christianity. The God, the substance, that he talked of is the infinite, the absolute. Spinoza's problem, though, is how to explain variety. The Judaeo–Christian formulation of the dilemma is that there is one substance that is eternal and infinite, and the rest of the world that we see around us is dependent on that one infinite reality. Neither formulation is right. In each case, it's the best approximation that can be

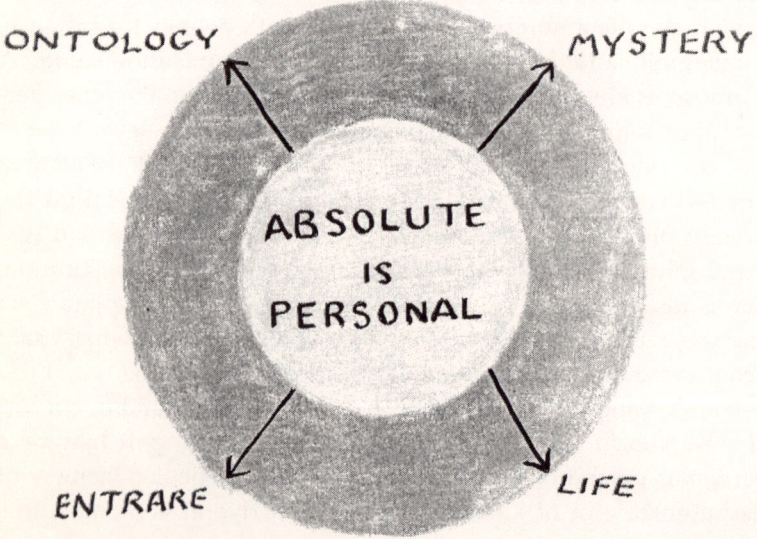

managed. It is a problem the human mind can't grasp. It may be that if we evolve, we may be able to grasp it in another two million years' time, if we have not blown ourselves up before then. So "ontology" is the scientific method for trying to understand this central matter. I have used the word *entraré* to mean entering into this matter through intuitive understanding. It is the word used by the philosopher Vico, who has been championed in the English-speaking world by Isaiah Berlin. Vico believed that human beings have a special faculty for entering into an understanding both of each other as individuals and also of each other's cultures.

The other point is about life itself. We are all, unfortunately, absolutely saddled with a view that we are all driven by instincts. Now, the whole instinctual theory doesn't really fit *living* beings—not only human beings, but all living organisms. We all have instincts within us, but the essence of ourselves consists in a generative capacity within the organism enabling it one way or another. I have been in correspondence recently with Elliott Jaques, who has been writing on this subject. He believes that even the amoeba actually isn't absolutely determined in that if a bit of food comes down one way or another, it can sort of say, "I like this bit of food rather than the other." It is quite central to the religious viewpoint that there is an intentional something that originates from within the living being. In all the great religions there is a reward for acting one way rather than another. The instinctual theory is that we are driven from without. Of course, we are affected by what comes from without, but we are not under *necessity*, as are the elements in the inanimate world.

This same duality is within the human being.

We are the absolute. The other is in us, and the person is a creative centre; then there is another side, which I put down as self-centred narcissism, psychosis, autism. It may be a little too simplistic, yet I think nearly all psychiatric conditions can be simplified down to something much more elemental. Think of them either as processes or a pattern that interferes with the capacity of the person to have understanding and freedom.

All great religious thinkers have been in touch with this dual current running within us. In their struggle to get in touch with the absolute, the great religious genii have separated themselves from other human beings. Moses had his enlightenment alone on the top

DUAL CONSTITUTION OF THE PERSONALITY

THE ABSOLUTE
THE OTHER
THE PERSON

SELF CENTRED
NARCISSISM
PSYCHOSIS
AUTISM

of Mount Sinai. Jesus faced the dark horrors in himself out in the desert. The Buddha left his wife and his child in the palace and found enlightenment alone in the Deer Park, and it was the same with Mohammed. But the place where we meet the absolute today is through encounter with the other. We are rooted in the other, and we make contact with it through a direct confrontation with another person. The transference interpretation is central in psychoanalysis for that reason.

We all resist acts of understanding. It's rather well known that within psychoanalysis we resist understanding, but it was only when I was coming to study this a bit more that it suddenly struck me that it's not just within psychoanalysis that we resist understanding, but that this is only one instance of a much more general resistance. In other words, we resist *all* acts of understanding. As soon as you understand something, it puts a totally new demand upon you, and this is so even with scientists. Keppler, when he discovered that the planets went around the sun in elliptical orbits and not in circular orbits, waited for six years before he revealed it, because he felt he was destroying something beautiful—a picture of perfection. But it's not only that. We all resist acts of understanding: they place a burden upon us; we are not the same after we've had an act of understanding. It changes us; we are different persons.

You probably all know Piero della Francesca's painting of the Baptism of Christ—this is one of the examples I thought was quite illuminating. I looked at it fairly carefully in the National Gallery

two or three days running, and in the figure of Christ you can see in his downcast eyes the burden upon him of what's happening. I may be imagining this, but I think when you look at the original you can see in his eyes resentment too, as if he knew and hated what was being put upon him. But I take this as a symbol. It's an external picture of an inner realization—a dramatic representation of an inner realization. This is something we very much want to resist, because it changes us; we are not the same afterwards. That's why I think in rituals where someone is anointed—as in the coronation of the monarch, for instance—a very heavy duty is imposed. The ritual is the external sign of which the inner correlate is an act of understanding. It makes sense of something that has surprised me very much in recent years: where a patient has a remarkable insight, which she gives voice to, and the next time I see her, she'll say: "You know that thing you said the other day..."—but it wasn't what I had said, it was what she had understood and herself expressed. I don't say it hadn't come about as a result of an interaction between us, but nevertheless it was her insight. I can think of times when I've thought, "My heavens, that's interesting, I'd never have thought of that", and then the next time the insight has been attributed to me. Quite striking. I think it's for this reason, that once the person really has an insight and an understanding, her path can't be the same, and there is a fear of it and a desire to offload it onto another. It relates to what I will discuss later—which is conscience and freedom.

I just want to end by trying to get across what I think is the importance of this: two things, really. One is that this is, I think, the root of understanding the way human beings operate psychologically, and there is a great deal of talk in the literature that we've got a very mechanistic model—all that is true, but that's the negative way of viewing things. I think all that comes about as a result of not having the basic ontology that is there first. If you have that, then the mechanistic viewpoint hasn't got a place. If you grasp the ontology lying behind acts of understanding, then mechanism just fades away.

I just want to end with a vignette.

Joan, my wife, and I went to a lecture given by an American woman who is a teacher in Sydney, but she'd been trained in the States and she went back there on a six-month sabbatical; the way she put it was this: "When I was at school as a girl, we used to be told off if we dropped sweet papers on the ground, or if we ran down a corridor, and so on." When she went back 25 years later, all the students had to be frisked to make sure they didn't have guns in their pockets; teachers were terrified of marking someone down in exams because they might get mugged on the way home. The whole scene she painted was horrific. But the interesting thing was this: she immediately said that "Obviously what has happened here is a collapse of values", and then she was in a dilemma and she half moved towards getting back into a fundamentalist type of position, but she also realized that it couldn't be the answer. The world splits into this very fundamentalist type of solution on the one hand and, on the other, a chaos, but a new type of understanding is possible. There can be a religious and psychological way of living that relates to others in their intimacy. The thing I want to try to get across is, you see, that these things actually affect the fine detail of how one speaks to patients.

* * *

Floor: Well, that was music to my ears, I must say. I'm a Jungian, and one of the reasons I'm a Jungian really is because of Jung's belief in the religious principle within all human beings, so it's absolutely lovely for me to hear you from a different tradition and orientation speak in this way, and I'm sure you will have many differences from the way Jung puts it, as I do, certainly, but just hearing that was very good for me.

Also, your concentration, your bringing out the necessity of speaking in simple and old-fashioned language, I liked very much, and I wanted to bring up a point that is made by James Hillman in his book, *The Myth of Analysis,* in which he makes a very interesting and very controversial point, I think. He's talking about resistance. I'm going to say this badly because I can't in fact remember exactly what he says, I haven't got the words entirely in my head, but he says something like, "Resistance is to the analyst's love, resistance in the patient is to the analyst's love." This, of course, is typically James Hillman, he's a bit of a wild card and a bit of a maverick, even in Jungian circles, but I think it's a very profound and courageous point and causes a lot of controversy. But I think he's indicating the same sort of thing that you are suggesting. He's obviously not talking about eroticized love, but it's that kind of attempt at intimacy that he's talking about, and I just wondered if you would comment on that.

Yes, I'll comment on both. The first thing I just want to go back to is one of the great disasters in the psychoanalytic world, which is what I call "splitting by whole objects"—Freud is good, Jung is bad, Melanie Klein is good, Kohut is bad, etc. It's a disaster, and I think it relates to George Orwell's point about the effort that is required not only for expressing what one thinks but for thinking itself. It is more effort to think out and discriminate the good from the bad or the good from the irrelevant, and so on.

I think Jung was right when he said in *Modern Man in Search of a Soul* that the basic problem for every person over the age of 35 a religious one. However, I feel very antipathetic towards what he says in his book *Psychology and Religion*, and I'll tell you why. He espouses that particular form of religion which endorses or puts value upon submission of the individual to an awe-filled God, and it's the central issue in his paper. I stress the fact that we participate in the infinite because the kind of submission that Jung preaches is not possible if you understand religion in the way I have been trying to elucidate. I see religion as generating the personal and creative. To equate religion with submission is a disaster in itself, but it's even more dangerous in Jung's *Psychology and Religion* for another reason.

When he begins to describe what it is to which one submits and how you *know* what the truth is, he says it's the *consentium gentium*, which means what is believed by the majority—which is a most alarming statement. I think Erich Fromm, in his little book *Psychoanalysis and Religion*, is quite right in his criticism of Jung on this point, because he says that once you take that view, you could say that in Germany Nazidom was the truth because it was in the majority. Fromm says that we all know about a *folie à deux*, but we can also get a *folie à millions*. Fromm's instancing of Nazi Germany may be an extreme example, but it's where Jung's view can lead you. So that side of Jung is very unfortunate, and I would hope that all Jungians would really address themselves to it with healthy self-criticism. When I had written that chapter of the book, I sent it off to Louis Zinken, who was still alive at the time, and I asked him for his view of it. He wrote back: "Yes, I know Jung does say that in *Psychology and Religion*, but I don't think he meant it!" But, you see, even that worried me a bit because I think one must try to avoid making gods out of these people. Jung did make mistakes. To put the other side of Jung, which comes out in his *Answer to Job*, I think what one might call his demythologization of God is a marvellous piece of exegesis. But I personally do think that one has to be very careful of making submission to an outer authority as central as Jung does. In later life Jung took the view, and he actually said this, that he thought that Catholicism (and he's particularly espoused to Catholicism) and the other great traditional religions, were great psychotherapeutic systems, and he recommended some of his patients to reconvert to their religion. All that worries me a bit too, because it seems too undiscriminating, and so I think the view that Jung is the one that one looks to be the psychological advocate for religion is a mistake. I am critical of Erich Fromm for a particular but different reason. He thinks that the religious principle endorses the idea that a person is the centre of his own sort of potentialities and has the courage to create from it. This is the exact opposite of Jung's view, and I think Fromm, rather than Jung, should be our advocate for religion within psychology. His approach, which is more internal and centred upon the person's inner creativity and courage, is a better religious template for our age.

There is the other question of the resistance to the analyst's love. My slight worry about it is this. It's quite common, this sort of view within psychoanalysis and psychotherapy that if you ask someone, "How does the patient's ego become strengthened?" you will very often get the answer that it's the analyst's validating them or supporting them and creating the right environment that strengthens the ego. All those things *favour* change but do not of themselves bring it about. What strengthens someone's ego is an act from within. So, in answer to the point from James Hillman, the act might be the overcoming of a resistance in one's self, making a generous response to the analyst's care. I would personally be happier if it were more based on the idea of a resistance to understanding.

When supervising, I have often said to the therapist, "How did you feel when this patient did this?" "Oh, I felt that he was trying to understand", or "I felt he was trying to . . ." "But, I'm not talking about that. How did *you* feel?" I gave an example, in *The Making of a Psychotherapist*, of a woman psychotherapist, who was Scottish, treating someone who was making a whole lot of very derogatory remarks about Scottish people—that they were mean-minded, ungenerous with money, etc.—so I said to her, "Well, how did you feel?" She said, "Oh, I felt he was trying to sort of get something." So I said, "But how did *you* feel?" So she said again, "Well I thought, you know, that he was trying to get some point across to me", and so I said, "But how did you *feel*?" and I still couldn't get an answer. I said then, "Listen, you're at a cocktail party and someone comes up and they start being very abusive to Scottish people." "I'd feel very angry." "Well, why weren't you angry there in the consulting-room?" I don't mean that the anger then had to be discharged, but that there was an anger there to be processed, and something be done with it. You see, I do think there is this unfortunate tendency to feel that when you get into the consulting-room, you step into some slightly non-human role, you don the cloak of God, you're not supposed to feel angry, and you're supposed to be loving on all occasions. That's the only thing that worries me a bit about the analyst's love. What if the analyst is not feeling love.

> *Floor:* I think he meant something rather larger and more objective by love.

Yes, I understand, I'm just giving you my slight worry about it.

> *Floor* [*next audience member*]: One of the things I welcome in this conference, and your courage in writing your book, I think, is to do with the numbers of us who I'm sure have kept our spirituality and our psychoanalytic practice quite separate, and so I have tried quite hard myself, particularly in the last year, I've just written a dissertation on spirituality in Kleinian psychotherapy. For me it was a very exploratory thing to do, because I knew it was there, and I wanted to clarify something that felt obscure to me. I think it was particularly in the area of faith and the good object, and I think that's where there is an area of great overlap between the act of faith in an

internalized good object and the act of faith that a lot of us have made in our spiritual lives, in whatever fashion. I mean, I have spent twenty years meditating and am very keen on contemplation, and there are two points I wanted to make to you. One is that there has been quite a long tradition of house-dwellers who have been meditating in their own family context. They haven't just separated off to seek God, but, in the Buddhist tradition, for example, there have been enlightened house-dwellers... there is a tradition of house-dwellers or house-owners, not only people who are hermits and solitaries, who seek God—that's just one point.

The other point is to do with what you call submission, but what I call surrender as opposed to submission; I really welcome your cautioning people about Jung's idea of what you call submission, but my own experience of contemplation and meditation is that what is referred to by surrender is to do with opening up the boundaries of the ego-self. Without an ego-self nobody could do that without enormous terror, and part of what I wrote in my dissertation is that I have found that, myself included, having done quite deep meditation, there came a point where there was a lot of fear about opening any further, and that was partly to do with paranoia, paranoid fears, and so on. I think analysis to a great extent helped with internalizing a good object and strengthening the sense of a good object. So in meditation, and in deep contemplation, I think what happens is that if you've had a long experience of analysis and facing your own fears, you can actually, with greater certainty and solidity and substance—a sense of strong ego, as it were—be willing to open up in meditation. That's an act of transformation in itself, and that, I think is what is meant by surrender to a good, loving principle. There is enough discrimination to see what is an act of surrender— to love—and what might be misguided and illusory, and I think it's very important to think about the uses and misuses of religion, and people who have not had very much experience of their own psyche using religion in all sorts of deluded ways. Anyway, I've said a little bit about my own interest.

OK. Look, I accept that, use of surrender . . .

> *Floor:* It's not surrender to another, but surrender to a living principle.

Yes, I understand that—that's a different way of using the word. No, I mean, I'm perfectly happy with that sort of use of it. I would just like to pick you up on one thing, because it just relates a bit to what I said about language. What do you think it really means when you say "internalizing a good object"?

> *Floor:* What I mean by that is a protracted experience, an exposure, to the humanity and the good will of the analyst, and taking that in, the concern, goodwill, absorption of an experience of thoughtfulness, of understanding in the analytic procedure, the analytic experience, which remains in the self once there has been an ending. I don't see that as different from the kind of testing that one might have in a different location. I'm not putting that very clearly, except that it's tested, it's real, it's a human exchange over a long period, which is taken in.

Yes, I'm not completely at ease with that . . .

> *Floor:* I mean, Klein herself talked about faith and the good object.

You see, I think the good object has to be created, and certainly in the analytic situation, if it's benign and satisfactory, the creation of that object will be facilitated. If the analyst is someone of good will—that will help a great deal towards the creation of a good object, but I don't think you actually internalize the good will of the other person; if you do, you'll have to tell me how that's done, what happens.

> *Floor:* I would actually say that it's not a creation but a revival, it's a revival of potentialities that are there in each person, so it's a reconnection to qualities . . . that are in yourself and in the other because we contain all of this, so it's a revival and a reconnection to the forces of generosity, beauty, love, goodwill, humour, benignness, whatever . . .

Yes.

Floor: . . . so, it's a reconnection, I would say, rather than a new creation, which is my way of thinking.

Even connecting is something that you actually do, and it seems to me it has to be something—it's not just like two points existing apart and then they come into contact. It does seem to me that something has to occur and, as it were, the qualities or elements may be there in the personality, but that something has to occur to create those into a new being. As long as when you talk about connecting you do mean that it's something that comes out of you, then I feel in agreement with you. Not that one would want to recommend it, but there are people who have had analysts and therapists who have been pretty poor, and yet they have managed to create something. I'm absolutely of the view that some sort of goodwill and integrity in the person of the therapist and analyst is terribly important, but I'm not of the view that it is *that* that strengthens the ego. It's just a subtle difference, but it produces the environment that allows it to occur.

Floor: Which is generative, you mean?

I come onto it more later. In my paper called "The True and the False God" (Appendix A), I say that it's when what I call the "false god" gets installed in the analyst (it can get installed in other people), but even if it's a good god that gets installed in the analyst, it tends to smother the capacity for the person to act for herself.

Patients who have seen me outside the consulting-room have noticed my character defects, and my conclusion is that that's been very helpful. The very interesting thing is that when a fault in my character has been noticed and then I've drawn attention to the fact that the person has noticed it, the usual reply is, "Oh, I didn't really mean it", and there is a very strong wish to deny it. I think part of the reason for this is that there is a strong need to keep the analyst a bit godlike. As soon as a person says of his analyst, "Well, actually, this isn't right", or "He's got a bit of a prejudice this way or that way", it means that that person starts to take more responsibility for themselves, and even take a bit of responsibility for the treatment. A patient might then begin to say to himself, "Well, perhaps I might have to correct this fellow." I'm just trying to correct any tendency to make the analyst godlike. I think it's quite good news if someone ends an analysis and they can see the dark and the light in their analyst.

> *Floor:* I've thought quite a lot about Winnicott's work and that area of transitional space. That idea of meditation is, I think, a very helpful word in the process that seems to happen at some point in an analysis, both in my own and with certain patients, where it is possible to, in a sense, both be in some sort of state of meditation where there is the capacity to hold the "not-knowing" by both oneself and by the patient. It does seem that often out of that does come from the patient that moment of "knowing", and it seems to me that so often one never gets there. It's those rare times when actually there is that potential or there is that capacity. Certainly a number of people who have written about religion and spirituality often seem to use Winnicott's work. I noticed you didn't yourself, but people like Meissner and Rizzutto use his work.

In answer to this question, I just want to say one thing: when I'm talking about the infinite and the absolute, that is not the same as what Winnicott meant by the true self. It's slightly difficult to get across what the difference is, but Winnicott meant by the true self what I refer to as the self that was generated out of the romantic tradition. What I'm talking about here—and I hope to goodness this will be understood correctly—it's that part of the personality that's been intuited by the mystics and the seers as being the infinite and the eternal. It's invested and it infuses the personality, but it's understandable within an act of understanding. An act of understanding is not something you can ever quite say has a colour or a taste or something like that, so there is that difference. Now to Meissner; there is a tragedy here because he is clearly a scholar and he says a lot of very important things, but he has a totally deterministic type of view, and then he's got this religious view, and they don't marry up. It means that he has a fideistic view of religion alongside this other, and he hasn't said to himself that a religious philosophy and outlook require him to redo this determinist philosophy. I don't know the reason for it, except I do know that quite a number of religious people have a sense of inferiority in relation to the so-called positivist scientists. They are the establishment at the moment.

MEDITATION TWO

Freedom and survival

It's always a bit complicated to know where to start. There are points on the circumference of a circle and so it's a dilemma to know where to start. This is entitled "Freedom and Survival". Now, of course, in the inanimate world there is no freedom. I'm not going into the area of microphysics, but in the ordinary inanimate world there's no freedom. A stone rolls down a hill because it was pushed by something. The defining element in living things is that there is a source of action from within, and quite how that can be is again mysterious, but it is so. There is a source of action from within, more so in what I'll refer to as motile organisms like animals and so on than in what biologists refer to as sessile organisms like trees and plant life.

It's a basic conflict that human beings do desire freedom, and I think everyone who comes to a consulting-room desires freedom, but there is also a strong fear of it—this is what one might call "the spiritual" in the individual. Bion said in many different ways that the psychotic part of the personality was much more active in the culture than is generally realized. My understanding of that is that what one might call the spiritual element was something that is hated. I reformulated Bion's classic paper about the psychotic side of the personality that attacks the sane side as the psychotic side attacking the spiritual. It seems to me that the spiritual is inextricably linked to the capacity to make decisions; by decisions I don't mean choosing this path rather than another, I mean decision in that type of rather deep realization type of sense.

Perhaps I need to give a quick example that I gave in my book on narcissism. When I was at the Tavistock, I went through a phase where I became interested in people like drug addicts or recidivist prisoners who had recovered from their condition and got better. I came across a fellow who had been a serious alcoholic and drug addict, and he had been in and out of prison. I asked him one day (and when I knew him he had recovered and he was married and had two children and seemed quite settled) what it was that had brought about the change, and there were some very interesting things that I have to leave on one side, but this is the crucial point that relates to here. He was in the alcoholic ward at the Friern Barnet, and they had a rule that if one of the patients went out and had a drink, they weren't allowed back in. Also, his wife had thrown him out, and he was never to come near the door of the house again or she would call the police. Anyhow, he went out of the ward, he went to the local off-licence, bought a couple of bottles of wine and drank them, and he came back and he sat on a bench at night in the grounds of the hospital, and it was pouring with rain. He had an empty bottle lying beside him, and he said to himself, "There are only two things I can do: Either I commit suicide, or I take this bottle and throw it through the windows" [of the alcoholic ward that he was in]. He was sitting there with rain pouring down, and he said that suddenly a very strange thought came to him. He said to himself, "Or I could decide to get better." Now, I tell that story because I think that that third thing was a decision—the first two weren't decisions. Only the third is what I call a decision. It's slightly odd because it came to him as an unexpected thought, and it confirms the point that Elliott Jaques makes that the actual moment of decision can't ever be reached, but the result of it can be experienced and felt. In a correspondence with Elliot Jaques I suggested that one shouldn't use the word "decision" because it's so misapplied, and instead use some word like "realization" or "inner illumination" or "new understanding". Following in a way what I have recommended myself about language, he said, "No, no, we should use the word 'decision' and reinvest it with its real meaning and push away the false meaning." I say this because I think many many things that are called decisions are not decisions at all. They are reactions. Thinking of that man—what was it, what was that something that moved in the depths? That thought was a creative thought, and so something that has been created in the depths. In my view, every thought is a creation. By thought I don't mean when you ingest and repeat a thought that has been communicated to you, but when something is generated from within as a thought, that's a creation. I think the fundamental difference between a thought and a feeling is that a feeling is not a creation.

Now, just to repeat what I said when I was talking about that woman: the question is "why is it feared", and there is no doubt that it is feared, and I think the reason is the moment that I have a truly creative thought I get a bit more self-knowledge and it's a bit of self-knowledge that may be very uncomfortable. I think that is one of the reasons that it is resisted. One of the things that I think is terribly important—and it does come out of what I call "the good religious tradition"—is that a truly creative thought is closely related to conscience. It's a rather surprising thing that in the field of psychoanalysis and psychotherapy, conscience is not used very much; but, again, one of the reasons is that conscience is associated with the superego and that's a disastrous mistake. They are two totally different things—in fact, the superego smothers conscience. In the paper called "An Exegesis of Conscience in the Works of Freud" (Appendix B), I try to show that actually the way Freud uses conscience is almost synonymous with the superego; there are some exceptions, and it's slightly sad—in a couple of papers he clearly has a different view, but it then seems to get smothered over again. The architect of that idea of conscience as an inner figure that condemns came from St Paul, and it was quite striking for me to realize that Freud and St Paul had the same idea of conscience. It was surprising with Freud's very anti-religious attitude that in fact he took up St Paul's view. I can't go into the full history of it, but it is related to the way the idea of God and a mechanistic universe and so on came to be. I think one of the problems in almost all the great religious traditions is a conservatism, a dogmatism, that strangles the operation of conscience. And of this I am absolutely certain, that a great deal of psychotherapy and psychoanalysis strangles it also and you get two types of different positions—there's what I call a "bad god" that condemns, and very often the analyst gets into that position and even from a benign point of view overrules conscience; the other way is analysts who allow a type of condemning god to remain inside the patient, and so either it gets installed in the analyst, who then operates from it, or there is a type of analyst who leaves the persecuting god inside the patient. In both cases conscience gets overruled and is smothered.

One of the great treasures that was bequeathed upon the world by Judaism was that it was here in the ancient Israelites that conscience came to birth in a way that was not so in the East. It seems to me to be one of the most extraordinary events in human history that here is this small tribe wedged between the great empires of Egypt, Assyria, and Babylonia, conscience came to birth. It was the genius of this people that placed conscience almost as its political charter. King David, musician, military general, political genius, as you all know, committed a deed that we would consider vile: he took the wife of Uriah the Hittite and he slept with her and made her pregnant (I am shortening the story, which I hope you might re-read), and he ordered his general Joab to put Uriah at the forefront of the battle so that Uriah the Hittite was killed. This was a vile deed, yet in fact it would have been quite acceptable to any Middle Eastern despot at the time—and, I might say, not only Middle Eastern despots but political despots in our own time. However, not for King David. The prophet Nathan came and spoke these words to David: "In the same town there were two men, one rich the other poor. The rich man had flocks and herds in great abundance. The poor man had nothing but a ewe lamb. One only. A small one that he had brought up, and he fed it, and it grew up with him and his children, eating his own bread, drinking from his cup, sleeping on his breast" and the Bible says "it was like a daughter to him. When there came a traveller to stay with the rich man, he refused to take one of his own flock or herd to provide for the wayfarer who had come to him, and instead he took the poor man's lamb and prepared it for his guest." David's anger flared up against the man: "As Yahweh lives", he said to Nathan, "the man who did this deserves to die. He must make fourfold restitution for the lamb for doing such a thing and showing no compassion." And then Nathan said to David, "You are the man." Then David says, quite simply, "I have sinned against Yahweh." I would prefer to translate that and say he'd sinned against his own conscience, and he knew immediately that he had done wrong. I think it's a very beautiful story, because Nathan doesn't come and say: "You've done wrong, my fellow." He tells him a story, and David says, "This is awful", and then he says, "This is you." It's quite a different way of saying things from saying: "You are a shocking fellow, look what you've done." David's own judgement came to operate, and I would feel quite happy as a psychoanalyst if I could make an interpretation like that. In order that conscience might operate, it is necessary for the person to make their own judgement (I have written a paper on this—see Appendix C). If you point out to someone "Look, it seems clear that what you are doing is very envious", not many people won't hear that as being, "—and you shouldn't be". My own view is that it is no good putting it that way. It needs instead to be understood what the psychological activity called envy is; actually forget the word and make yourself understand what it is, then you might be able to describe that—and in fact it is something that will always be injurious to the person himself or herself. The prophet's words would have had no effect had they not found an echo in King David's heart—in other words, his conscience operating, whereas most despots would have had the man executed. Just as in China there developed a tradition of balanced living through the philosophy of Confucius, so, after David's reign, there followed a tradition of prophets whose job was to keep alive the faculty of conscience in the people.

It may be controversial but it's probably worth saying that this insight into the functioning of conscience arose, I think, through a spiritual genius in the ancient Israelites. It is in fact one of the great endowments of our civilization, and it was the product clearly of a human creative understanding; in my view it flows from that part of a personality that I refer to as the infinite. In any form of argument you have to make some leaps, and the leap I make is that conscience is the subjective experience of the infinite within the personality. But one of the tragedies in both Judaism and Christianity was that this became attributed to an almighty God who dictated, and I think that was quite mistaken. It happened in

Judaism, it happened in Christianity and in fact it happened in all the eastern religions. When the Buddha was dying, he said, "Don't take any of my tenets because I said them, exert them to evidence." That was the Buddha, but it wasn't too long before he was made basically into a god. Jesus was specifically made into a god. Mohammed, although not theologically, has effectively been made into a god, and the whole Salman Rushdie episode sort of proves it, really. But as soon as that happens, you get the position of "I mustn't do this because I am told not to", and as soon as that comes into play, conscience gets smothered. One of the great Roman Catholic theologians in the last century, Cardinal Newman, who was a convert from Anglicanism to Roman Catholicism and then became a cardinal, said in his writings: "If I had to decide between what the pope said and my conscience it would always be my conscience", and he was one of the great paragons of the Catholic church. But it's rare.

I want to say a bit more about the way conscience came to be understood at the time of the Enlightenment. If the analyst or therapist is installed as God—and he very often is, and there is a terrific drive on the part of the patient to cast him in this role due to this fear of human freedom—and so, if responsibility for making one's own judgement can be pushed out onto the other, as often happens, it destroys conscience. But what I call the Pauline idea of conscience as a condemner—even a condemnation for the act itself—would not be too bad, but (and I'll come to this more when we get onto the pattern of madness) the problem is that people nearly always hear any statement like that as "and see what a rotten fellow you are." That is nearly always how it is taken, and my own view is that many, many, many interpretations are taken as declarations confirming the individual's conviction that he is a rotter, and this prevents the person from making his own judgement. You know, if you're absolutely rotten and hopeless, then it doesn't encourage you to get up and do anything, especially to be responsible for your own judgements. But at the time of the Enlightenment, led particularly by Rousseau, the structure of traditional religions began to disintegrate, and so what I call "natural religion" came into play, and conscience took centre stage. Conscience now came forward as an invitation not as a condemnation. It seems to me absolutely elemental that conscience is always an

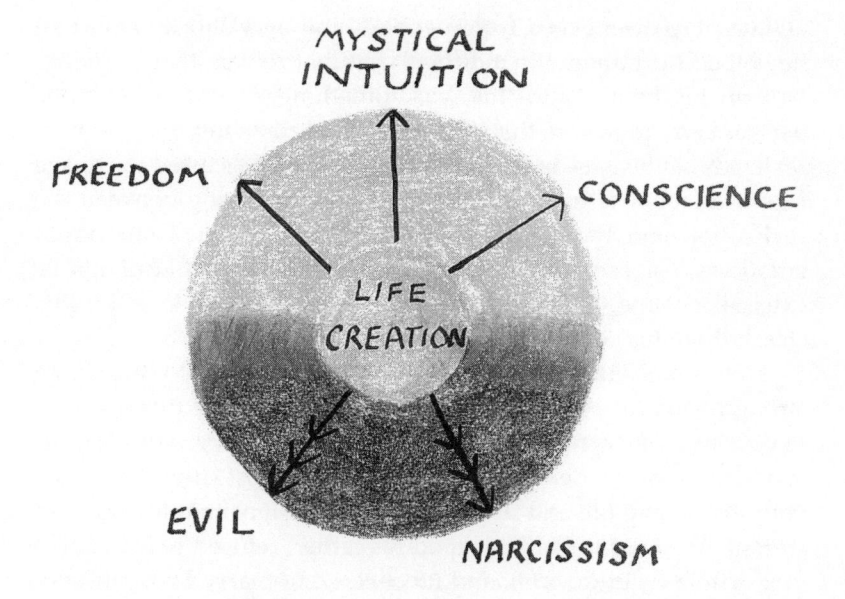

Diagram: A circle labeled "LIFE CREATION" at center, with arrows pointing outward to "MYSTICAL INTUITION" (top), "FREEDOM" (upper left), "CONSCIENCE" (upper right), "EVIL" (lower left), and "NARCISSISM" (lower right).

invitation, and if you reflect on your own experience and the doubt about whether to do this or that, conscience is always an invitation. Therefore when it is repudiated—that's why I come back to the idea of the infinite in which we all share—it's a repudiation of something that is basic to our nature, and our human task is to allow the infinite, the absolute, to become that which permeates our nature.

I might just give a clinical example here. Matthew came to see me because his girlfriend, Bonita, had sent him. After a time, I pointed out that he was degrading himself really with this mythology, and it was quite clear that he was coming on his own account. He was very threatened by this awareness, and then he said, "I realize how withdrawn I am and how I always stay disengaged from people." He realized this was something he was doing. The point I am making here is that any interpretation that is really effective has to bring conscience into play, because an interpretation really is a statement. So you might ask, "Well, what is the purpose of making a statement?" The reason is that conscience then starts to invite the person to do something. It's quite interesting: this man said, "I realize how withdrawn I am and how I always stay disengaged from people", and very shortly after that he helped his father with a difficult family problem that the father had on his hands, and this was something he had never done before. I am quite sure that conscience had come into play, that he realized that he was disengaged, and so when he started to engage it was a response to conscience. There is something between the realization and the action. I look at it more when I talk about emotions. You see, most of morality is based on what I call mobile external actions, whereas emotions are invisible actions, and so clearly here his conscience was active.

I am quite certain that this man's active response to conscience strengthened his ego. I'm not saying that it was just that, but this understanding crystallized various things. It had strengthened his ego—he'd always deferred to people in the most disastrous way, both in his love life and in practical affairs. Signs that his ego had strengthened were that he helped his father, refused to lend some money to a ne'er-do-well, and he decided to marry his girlfriend. He had been in state of panic about any type of engagement with anyone until then. I am pretty certain that if I had taken the line of saying how disengaged he was, this wouldn't have happened. He made that judgement about himself. If I had said to him, "You know, you're very disengaged in the way you carry on", the implication again is: "You shouldn't be, you know. That's not the right way to be. Mature people engage, you know, especially me." It's a very subtle thing, but it's terribly important. Sometimes after a session I have taken a pad of paper and actually tried to work out ways of saying things so it is just a statement—otherwise we rob the person of his chance to exercise his own judgement.

To give you an example of where I didn't do this, I once said to this patient: "I noticed that you were more thankful and warm last session than normal, and I think it was because you were grateful that I had identified a frightened handicapped child inside you the session before." Does that sound all right to you? What's wrong with it?

Floor: ... normality, the reference to "normal", the implication she wasn't like that before.

Yes, the offending words were "more than" and "normal". Luckily—when we talk about patients that are good to learn from—she noticed it, of course, and then the next session she came back and remonstrated with me. But the simple thing, the right thing to have said, would have been: "I think you were grateful that I had identified a frightened and handicapped child last session." I was fortunate with that particular patient that her central problem, which she knew and understood, was deferring to God as opposed to actually following what she felt, so it was immediately picked up by her. She came with that problem, and she was sophisticated enough to know that that was her problem. In a previous treatment there had been a type of imposition.

I think with people who are in this field, particular care needs to be taken over people who decide to train, for instance, it's so easy for it to be a very good profession for you to be in. Once I had the experience of a woman who decided suddenly to take up psychology, which seemed quite alien to her line of interests. Her own field was remote from it, and she seemed terribly agitated and anxious about it; she started going to psychology lectures, which she found very uncongenial. Then I made this interpretation to her: "I think you believe that I'm looking into a mirror and I've fallen in love with my own reflection, and you believe that unless you conform to that reflection, you won't get any interest from me." Shortly afterwards she gave up psychology. I think it's terribly important to try to get hold of and allow conscience to function inside the person, not to rob him or her of a chance to make a judgement.

Getting back to this thing of language—in "Lines of Advance in Psycho-Analytic Therapy" (1919a [1918]), Freud said, "You can analyse the elements inside a person but the actual job of bringing them together and making something, that's nothing to do with the analyst", and he referred to it as "the synthetic function"; I prefer to call it the operation of conscience. I think what conscience invites someone to do is to draw in the different parts of themselves and make them into a whole. The human person is a creation, it's not given. As soon as something is condemned, it is split off, and then the individual hasn't got all the parts of themselves available, the parts that they need to make themselves into a full human person. I do think that there are two ways in which that happens. One is for the analyst to get installed as the condemner, but the other is for the condemner to stay inside. I won't refer to different schools of thinking or different clinical schools, but I can think of clinical schools where I have seen quite clearly the person installing themselves in the god position and condemning; I've also seen the other, where the person is bending over backwards to say to the person, "Oh, you're all right, really", and that's just as bad, because the inner condemning god remains in place, undealt with and not dissolved.

> *Floor:* I was just very struck with how the things you were saying could very much apply to the dichotomy of Eros and the death instinct. I'm thinking of the death instinct in terms of returning to the inorganic, where nobody can make a decision and nobody can move.

Well, I'll tell you my difficulty about that. I haven't said quite enough about the business of survival—I think one of the problems is that we are under the Darwinian dogma, which is that our basic drive is for survival. It is always there and Jonathan Bradley said at the beginning that if there were a fire, we would all have to get out.

> [*Jonathan Bradley*: Not immediately!]

Well, we'd think about it first! We'd all have to get out, and so it's clear that there are moments when our survival is threatened, and then the instincts come into play. This is slightly to reduce the way of trying to explain this, but I do think it's very important. The instincts are those things that drive us. If you like, they are the inanimate within the human organism, but they're not the area of relevance usually in human interaction. I will use the analogy of gravity to stand for instincts. If someone came in that door and said, "Why are all these people sitting here?" and you answered, "Well, the reason is that there is a particular law that Newton discovered called gravity; there is a certain big mass and it exercises a force of attraction and that keeps all these people in these seats, and if it wasn't for the fact of this gravity, then they would be floating up in the air." That's perfectly true; it's not actually relevant though. It's not untrue, and it's a perfectly valid answer, but it's not actually relevant because the relevant answer is that this group is here in order to enter into a communicative dialogue on certain subjects. This is a little bit simplistic, because I think the thing is a bit more complicated in terms of history and development of civilizations. There's always a pendulum movement between survival and culture. It's always appeared to me one of the strange dilemmas that you usually get some shocking monster warrior who goes and conquers a whole lot of territory, and once he has conquered it and put big walls around it, then a civilization can build up in relative peace. But then, of course, as soon as that is threatened—the survival instinct comes back into play—so I am not denying the existence of the survival instinct. As Bion said once, "Patients always, always come to the consulting-room because they want something more than survival." A cynical analyst would say that it is masochism, but there have been heroes who have decided to choose death rather than go in another direction. There was that plane that crashed in Gerona; luckily no one was killed, but a man and his wife got out, and then the man heard children screaming, and he ran back into the plane. How do you explain that on the basis of the survival instinct? Now, there are people who'll argue it like this: that if he went and got the children out, that would advance his reputation, and it would help him, and so on, but I think it's pushing it a long way. I don't think that the instinctual way of describing things is helpful, and what I think actually needs to be done is a whole theory of psychotherapy and psychoanalysis based on an understanding of human communication.

Now, to come to the death instinct: I have a shrewd suspicion that Freud half knew this, because the death instinct is not an instinct in any ordinary sense of the word; hunger, sex, thirst, desire for protection, these are instincts. He could have said that there's a process of disintegration going on, but I don't think instinct is even the right word for what he is describing. I think Freud was honest enough, when he experienced the whole business of traumatic dreams during the First World War and the repetition compulsion, to re-do his theory and say, well, this instinct theory was not good enough; and so he brought in Eros and the death instinct. I think you could remove the word "instinct" from those two: Eros means that sort of principle that brings people into connection with each other, and the death instinct means destructive forces and disintegration. I am not saying that we don't all have instincts. I'm thirsty, and so I have a glass of water. But you don't get a human psychology until you get a response to that, and a human creative response is at the moment you get a human psychology. There have been people who have been hungry and decided to let themselves not have food, like the people who have gone on the hunger strikes in the Maze Prison, and so on. I think that there is a sort of Darwinian dogmatism where you attempt to explain all human endeavour in terms of a struggle for survival, and I just don't think that is true. It's where what I call the religious model comes in and says that there is something else. All the great religions have put emphasis on the fact of human choosing, and it can mean that they can choose against the instincts, among other things.

> *Floor:* Some of the things you said started a train of thought in me that I thought it might be a good idea to check with you that it hasn't gone completely wrong. When you were talking about conscience and the fact that it was eventually invested with god in a prescriptive authority...

Yes, not that conscience became invested with that, but that this process occurred which actually smothers conscience.

> *Floor:* Yes. I think that for me is what brought up the distinction between religion and spirituality, because religion is prescriptive, it is about how should you be. I think—at least, this is my understanding, of course I may be wrong here—but the way I understand it is that it tries to tell you that if you are afraid of taking your freedom, or if you don't know how to go about becoming a human being, then follow this path, and this is the right path to follow. Now it may be that at some stage of your personal development you can actually find the spiritual core of religion, but as a starting point it may be that religion is not such a bad thing.

Yes. I'm not against religion; part of the point I'm getting at is that the great religious traditions have these pearls of wisdom inside them. I'm not against that. It's also true that socially a whole lot of prescriptions have to be laid down. It's because if you try to plan and make rules and regulations, it's just not possible, as any lawyer knows, to be subtle enough, and so it's a rough, crude type of prescription: you know roughly this is what you should all do. That's where when you talk about religion you mean that aspect of it, but it's very rough and crude; actually, as Newman said in one of his treatises on conscience, "I can no longer think, I can no more think with someone else's mind than I can eat using someone else's hand"; in the same way with conscience, what he's getting at there is that the thing is much more subtle, and so the broad lines can be drawn out: "Thou shalt not murder", and "Thou shalt not do this", and so on, but they are just very broad categories. As people have pointed out, conscience may come into play not necessarily between a good and an evil, but between two goods, even, or a person may have to make a judgement as to which they feel is the better in these circumstances. So, if you are talking about religion in the sociological sense and laying down certain general principles, I think you are right, obviously, about that. But the problem is when the prescription gets invested with what I call godlike qualities: "This is what you must do." Let's think of a simple example: you know you must stop at a red light, but if I had someone in the car who suddenly had a heart attack and I was trying to get them to hospital, I'd have no doubt the thing would be to go through the red light as long as I wasn't going to injure anybody.

Floor: Wouldn't you say that this is more a political, power issue that applies both to religion and the therapeutic encounter, that the use of prescriptive language or prescriptive ideas is often done to subtly obtain power. When you are talking about religion, it's over a population; when you are in therapeutic encounter, it is over the patient.

It may be used that way, but it may not. In most of the psychotherapy world there's an agreed type of understanding that sessions last fifty minutes and so on, and that's a sort of prescription. In fact, I would think it was a mistake if it became invested with godlike type of qualities. I had an example at the Tavistock once: I was seeing a woman in mental distress, and the session came to an end, but she refused to leave and I got a bit hot under the collar about it, and then I thought, well, actually, I don't need the room for the next half-hour, so I left, and she left shortly after. This is quite illustrative: I was seeing her four times a week, and I didn't need my room straight away, and so for quite a period at the end of the session I went out of the room, and actually I think she needed the time to recover a bit. She was very distressed, and she nearly always left within five to ten minutes. But the illustrative point is this: it then happened—let's say it was a Tuesday—that I needed the room because there was a seminar or something straight afterwards, and I asked her if on Tuesdays she wouldn't mind leaving, and she left without demur. I knew perfectly well why: she didn't want to leave because "this is what you must do". As soon as she realized that it was a human need on my part, there was no problem. So, in answer to your question, something like that could be used to exercise power. I do remember that when she first said that she would not leave, I got agitated, and then I settled down in myself and thought that there was no reason why I shouldn't leave the room and let her stay there for a while.

An afterthought

When I said that the mystics went aside from the human community, it is this problem of trying to grasp how it is that we are made up of something absolute, infinite, and at the same time something individual that is particular to me, and yet the two things are in some way a unity—it is mysterious. I feel that there is something not fully understood, which is how we make contact with that—the infinite, the eternal. It is the same thing that Bion referred to as O—and, incidentally, quite a lot of people have thought that Bion's theory of O was a mystical type of romanticism, which he developed in his old age, when he was beginning to become senile. I have heard quite a number of people say that of his three great books, *Learning From Experience* and *Elements of Psychoanalysis* were marvellous, but that in *Transformations* he was beginning to go off. It was in *Transformations* that he first elaborated his idea of O. When Bion defines O, he says, "I mean by this godhead, the infinite, the ultimate, the absolute, those are the sorts of terms I mean when I use it." His idea of O is, in fact, integral to the rest of what he said, and if you dismiss that and say "well, I can accept some of those other things", you haven't really understood his theory—and of that I am absolutely convinced. The thing that he didn't do was to state that this overthrows a whole lot of the other theoretical positions that are current within psychoanalysis. The difference really in the way of thinking that has come about throughout psychoanalysis and through psychotherapies that are based on it is that the way one makes contact with the ultimate is through a directness of contact with another person. That is what is new, and that's what I would call a new spirituality—and a spirituality that's appropriate for our present era. I think the only way to try and get some understanding of that is to meditate, reflect, and try to reflect on the nature of our own being, the nature of reality, until something starts to become clear.

MEDITATION THREE

A pattern of madness

If our task is to make contact with the infinite through an act of understanding, I must emphasize that this act of understanding is not just an intellectual act. Bion said this, although I have a suspicion that people haven't quite realized that he said it; he said that in order to have an act of understanding there has to be: (1) the intellectual grasp, an illumination; but he says also that there has to be (2) what he referred to as a move from PS to D. PS to D sounds a scientific type of business, but what he meant was from a paranoid way of looking at things—which basically means that you look at things as something that is outside and something that is hated outside or feared outside—to depressive, where you realize something inside. That is the basic religious position. He was saying that the scientific and the religious have to intersect; that the scientific act of understanding will only come if it's connected to what he referred to as a depressive state—that is, a state of concern—and this is not concern for the other but concern for the ultimate, or the infinite. Neither science on its own nor religion on its own will do the trick.

So what is the pattern of madness? What is madness? What is it? In my book on narcissism I use the phrase "narcissistic constellation", and I posited the idea in that book that what constitutes narcissism is a refusal of the infinite in our being, what at that time I referred to as "the life-giver". I've changed my way of thinking about it. It's the same idea, but it's like the refusal of this basic element out of which we are all constituted, and it is that which produces madness. I didn't elaborate this in that book. The "narcissistic constellation" is a fundamental pattern underlying all the different psychiatric conditions or mental illnesses.

I'll just give a simple example to show what I mean. In a lot of literature a distinction is made between borderline conditions and narcissistic conditions, and then when it's asked what the difference is between these two, the answer is this: the narcissistic condition is one where the person apparently functions very well on the surface but in fact is quite disturbed underneath, whereas in the borderline condition the disturbance is out in the open; it is manifest and obvious. In fact, these are not different things, but just two ways of looking at the same thing. It is a very common phenomenon for psychoanalysts to have one of these two situations. One is where the patient in the consulting-room behaves in a very model sort of way and seems to be quite reasonably normal and sensible, and yet everyone outside is saying "what in the heavens is going on, this person is in a terribly disturbed state and messing up all their relationships" and so on. The other is the opposite of that, where in the consulting-room the person is obviously in the most shockingly disturbed state and perhaps hallucinating and so on, but outside seems to be functioning perfectly normally. What I am trying to get at is that it depends from where you are looking, but the two are really the same condition. I only give that as an example, but I think that if one can begin to get hold of what I call an inner pattern, one can see that it generates all the different psychiatric conditions. It is one of the unfortunate things that psychoanalysis has been colonized to a certain extent by psychiatry, so that its own type of inner understanding has been crushed by the psychiatric machine. I don't mean not to let those categories influence the way one looks at things, but there is no sense of what is the inner type of spirit that has gone wrong that is producing all these different conditions.

All the varied elements of this pattern are in fact one, but the limitations of our minds prevent us from seeing the unity. In fact the only way we can get at it is through each of the individual things. Note the visual aid called Intensifiers. (Intensifiers—see frontispiece.) Look at the lower part—the circle and with a jelly in the middle and a crust on the outside, and then you've got "God" and opposite "God" "the worm", and then you've got "primitive hatred" and "glue", meaning a "glue-like" attachment down at the bottom. It doesn't really matter exactly where one starts, and in fact they all interact with one another. One has to try to grasp all these elements as part of the "narcissistic constellation" or "mad pattern". One has to grasp *why* it is and also see why any of these elements in that pattern are injurious to the personality. I say this because, for instance, one hears a great deal in psychoanalytic talk and discussion the use of the word omnipotence, but I very rarely hear it explained why omnipotence is harmful? It's more or less condemned as a sin, or so-and-so is arrogant. It is perhaps unpleasant for *me* if someone else is very arrogant, but it doesn't really explain quite why it is injurious.

I want to have another go at grasping that this sort of basic element that we all share is something that's held in common, not just with us, but with the reality of the whole universe. Imagine that you are treating a patient and you notice that whenever you make an interpretation that seems to be rather helpful, the patient is contemptuous and attacking, and you point that out. The question is this: What is the purpose of pointing that out? The common answer would be that it is attacking the analyst or attacking the process. There is no rule that says the person can't attack the analyst, so there is no particular point in pointing that out. Attacking the process, that's perhaps a little bit better, but it doesn't really get to things; but if you take the view that the analyst as Other symbolizes the person's own elemental being, then it makes sense, because what you are actually witnessing tells you that the person is in fact attacking their own soul, as it were. But it requires quite a lot of processing in order to get at this. I can think of someone who whenever I said something that I thought was reasonably helpful would say, "I think I'll go off to another analyst." A lot of people wouldn't agree with this, but I didn't say anything about that; didn't say anything about it for a very long time, and it kept on happening. The person is quite free to say that, and it is one of the contractual arrangements in an analysis that the person can say what they want. The second thing is that if one comes in and says something about it, the person will assume that you are saying it because you are hurt by it. It is one of the principles of narcissism, or madness, that if I am hurt by something, then you must be too. As soon as you say something like that, the person will immediately take the view that the analyst is hurt, and that will also induce a certain amount of triumph inside a person. And it also does something else, because one of the ways that people become deified paradoxically is when there is an unconscious perception that the person is themselves very sensitive and easily hurt. The analyst is a symbol of the person's own psyche, and this truth alters the whole way one approaches the treatment of someone. I say this because I have listened to numerous presentations and just recently read two public clinical papers. In both these papers from people of quite different orientation there was an immediate jumping on the fact that an attack had been made. The clear implication is that this shouldn't have been done. I think a lot of psychoanalysis and a lot of psychotherapy is done on the basis of reacting far too quickly to the actual events rather than realizing what the thing is and then processing it and then bringing it up or using it later. The significance of the analyst being attacked is that it indicates that the person's own creative core is being attacked.

To get back to the pattern of madness: that looks a fairly simple pattern, and it is quite simple, but I think it's possible to understand madness and its core by understanding the elements of that. I'll start with the "jelly". I can think of patients who make these sorts of remarks: I can think of a man who said, "When my girlfriend gets angry, I become a jelly inside", actually using that word. "I felt absolutely shattered and in bits after such and such happened" is a common way in which people express themselves, but it is the basic sort of idea, really, that inside we are a jelly, we are gelatinous, which means there's no centre of action, no centre of activity, there's no capacity within to create, because if you are a jelly inside it just means that you are moved by whatever happens at any particular moment.

Take my poem, called *Fish in a Shoal*:

A wave comes from the left
And that's the way I move
My tail is a rudder
But currents are a pilot that decide every heading.
The currents are a pressure
That I am unable to resist
My tail can only move me
Quicker down their channels
I am their helpless victim.

A tone of voice, a raised eyebrow
A haughty manner or nose in the air
A suspicious look or a rude gaze
These are the currents that drive me
Along life's waterways.

I'm in a shoal with others
I feel their bodies swish
And I swirl with them all
They are the currents of my life
And there's no soul to resist.

So that's the jelly. Sometimes it's not obvious that the person in a state is "jelly-like", and this is because what is encountered is an outer rigidity—that's why I have got the crust. The difficulty of trying to express something in a design is that the jelly and the crust interact, so that when you see someone who is very rigid and dogmatic, you can always know that the jelly must be there. One of the values of looking at this pattern is that once you know and can begin to see that one of these elements is there, it is almost certain that all the others will be present.

If we take the idea that sanity is a state in which human beings are able to create, are able to create the elements in themselves into a person and to be free to be loving, then madness—this pattern (see Intensifiers: frontispiece)—is what prevents it and makes it not possible. The function of this whole system is to detach you from the basic element of your being, which is infinite. The other thing about it is that the whole pattern is senseless—if you try to work out a reason for it, that's what madness means—it is utterly senseless. I remember saying once to a woman, "I notice that when I give you a bad interpretation, one that will confuse and make things difficult for you, you embrace it, but when I give you one that is helpful you chuck it away", and she thought for a moment, and then she replied, "That's mad." I think it's a very good sign if you get that reply, because she sees that it is self-damaging and senseless. The nature of madness is that it is totally senseless. When I gave that example of the chap that was sitting outside the grounds of Friern Barnet Hospital, and those first two things he said: "I'll throw the bottle through the windows or I'll commit suicide", those are both utterly senseless, but also, one might say, they are reactive, that it's like the internal state is jelly-like. It's quite a simple idea, but it is quite difficult to realize that the person who is the most dogmatic, most definite, is always jelly-like, and the reason for that is that when someone is jelly-like, he takes in the imprint of the external stimulus. The stimulus response theory within psychology fits this system perfectly. That theory fits for someone in this narcissistic state, but not if sanity prevails. That's why I said that true thinking is creative—it comes from within— from the infinite. I have sometimes used this difference and it is like the difference, between taking a photograph of a scene as opposed to making a painting of a scene. This example is imperfect because I know photography is also an art, but if you just take the basic idea of the camera and you click and it records the scene, the jelly-like state leads to that sort of situation, so that we purely take in and what gets taken in becomes crust-like, and so whenever you meet dogmatism or rigidity, that's because things have been taken in, just like the jelly has taken an imprint, as it were, upon it. If someone has thought something out for themselves and it is something that they themselves have created, paradoxically they don't usually worry about it being criticized because it is too internal to themselves and they think, "Well, if the person wants to criticize it, then that's their business, they are entitled to their view." If, on the other hand, it's been taken in as an imprint, the person gets angry because underneath there is shame that they have not become a person but live in fakehood instead. Also, this crust is a protective wall around the jelly, and the individual feels his survival is at stake. I know also that if I criticize someone's analyst, I will not be liked. If that is so, it does mean that many things are ingested in this imprinted way, and this *has* to happen if the inner state is jelly-like

A PATTERN OF MADNESS

because there is no inner creative responsive principle that's able to sift—take in one thing, reject another or modify it, and so on.

The question is: let's say you meet someone in this gelatinous state, perhaps a patient —how to go about it? What exactly do you do? Some such patients have an insight but then later attribute it to the analyst or someone else. But there are many patients, and it has been written about quite a lot in the literature, who do sniff out the analyst's own attitudes, ways of thinking, and so on, and will ingest that, but it means that the state inside remains jelly-like. The question is how to deal with it. My idea is this: that I've got at the top there "intensifiers" and there are things within the personality that keep the jelly gelatinous and they keep the crust hard, and stiff, so, in other words, I use the idea of intensifiers that keep the crust hard, and then "liquefying" keeps the jelly in a liquid state. The question is, what are these "intensifiers"? Basically, they are made up of four very familiar things: greed, envy, jealousy, and omnipotence, or what I like to call "godlikeness". Quite an important thing here is that when we talk about greed or when we talk about envy or when we talk about jealousy, it is nearly always a definition that is based on my bad experience, and it doesn't necessarily refer to the person's subjective state or their own internal striving. A patient said this to me once: "I know it *looks* like greed, but I am in fact searching for something very desperately and I am terribly anxious not to miss it when it appears." I thought that was quite accurate, and it is true that it *looks* like greed, and in one way it *is* greed, but you need to grasp its inner meaning. That's one thing.

This business of the way you see it—it is more than just seeing it. It is the way in which you are able emotionally to receive it. I'll give you this example because it struck me very much at the time and has always stood as a symbol in my mind. I was seeing a woman who had had a psychotic breakdown, and she was in an isolated state, and when she first came into the consulting-room, she could only communicate the odd word. Slowly things developed, and she was able to communicate more. One day she came in very angry, and she said, "All you've taught me to do is to communicate with the wonderful you, and I can't communicate with anyone outside; I am isolated from everyone, and my life is an absolute misery. That's all you've done, to teach me to communicate with the wonderful you." Anyhow, the next day when she came, she said, "Now I've found someone who is really sympathetic to women." She was always complaining that I was unsympathetic to women's problems, which *may* have been partly true. Anyway, she said, "Now I have found someone really sympathetic to women's problems." She had been to see a gynaecologist, and she said, "He really listened, and I was able to speak to him, and the *difference* between him and you is just . . ." etc. I felt anger rising in me, and I was tempted to point out that she was rubbishing the work that we had managed to do. Luckily I didn't say that, and I calmed down, and then I thought "Aha!", and I said to her: "So, in fact since seeing you yesterday there has been some progress; you are now able to communicate not only with me but also with someone outside." Now, I keep that as a symbol, because, in fact, was it a destructive communication on her part or a constructive one? That depended to quite a large extent on the way that it was received. Do you understand what I mean? Often something that looks destructive is, in fact, constructive.

So, what I am trying to get at is that the "liquifiers"—greed, envy, jealousy, and godhood—keep the jelly gelatinous. It is terribly important that it is understood in such a way, that's why I call them the "liquifiers", because they are keeping the person in an inner gelatinous state with an outer crust.

The other thing is this: that greed, envy, and jealousy act in concert with one another. In the analytic literature people tend to differentiate between envy and jealousy. They are, of course, different, but I think it is a mistake to separate them because they *always* act in partnership together with greed. Now, this is the question: what essentially *is* greed? The word mustn't be used, but I think it is quite simple. As an aside, one of the unfortunate things is when we use words like greed—especially a word like greed—we tend to think of its primary meaning as existing in, say, someone who is greedy with food or money, but the primary meaning of greed lies in an emotional process of which greed for money or food are outer symbols. The emotional process of greed is taking in everything with violence. If any of you think, "I must take in *everything* that Neville Symington says", you will be in a disastrous state because the act of taking in has an implosive effect and keeps the jelly gelatinous. So much for greed.

The other thing is envy. The way Melanie Klein formulated envy was the idea that the person thrusts out—in the way she put it—their faeces into the breast, or the bad things inside them into the object, and that is the envious process. I think that is not the primary element in envy; it's what I call the second stage of envy. The first stage of envy is what's normally called in the literature "idealization". We have got to ban words like that because it doesn't actually tell you anything. When you talk about idealization, what does it mean? It has to mean that I *do* something if I perceive someone in an idealized way; I don't see the negatives in them and I see them in brighter colours than is really the case, and so I have to do something in order to have that perception. What I do is I get rid of my own good qualities and push them onto the other person, and that is why I have an idealized image. I push my own good qualities out, and those good qualities then obscure the bad qualities or the deficits in the figure that I am looking at. So in this situation we have greed operating, we have envy operating, we have the person imploding, taking into themselves far too violently a whole lot of stimuli and communications from the environment, and then at the same time they are getting rid of their own good things out into the figure or figures outside. Jealousy acts as a protective partner to the trio because it prevents any external influence coming in to modify it. The external influence in Freudian theory is thought of as the father, but in the way I like to think about it, what it keeps out is what I refer to as "the infinite" in the personality: it keeps that out so it, as it were, locks the person into a situation, so that these other two act the whole time so that things are sort of imploded into the personality and the good qualities in the person are got rid of, and that keeps the person in a jelly-like state both inside and then with a stiff crust on the outside. Obviously one must not be over-guided in a theory that one is going to follow willy-nilly. You have to go into your consulting-rooms and see whether you see that this is verified or not. There are signs, of course, as to whether someone is in this state or not. Are they very rigid? Are they very dogmatic? Do they complain about being exploited by people, and that they can't manage to stand up to them? Are they like that poem—exceedingly hypersensitive to any sort of criticism, and so on? If one sees these signs, one can begin to postulate that the rest of this system is in operation. I haven't even got on to "God", "paranoia", "the worm", and "the glue"—that will be for future meditations.

I think that Melanie Klein did us an enormous service in recognizing envy, but I don't think she recognized what I call the first stage of envy, and I also think that the definition of envy that she came up with was based on the analyst's bad experience. The intractability of what Melanie Klein called envy may in part be due to the condition being named "envy". The very naming of it as "envy" is a sign to some patients that the analyst is ruffled by this activity, and this becomes a secret triumph in the patient. "She must suffer from the same condition as me", says the patient in secret to herself. Of one thing I am quite certain: it is possible to interpret what I call the activity of these "liquifiers" (they also have the effect of petrifying as well, and petrifying has that double sense that the person is stone-like but also petrified), and it is related to panic. If it is possible to interpret these activities that are going on, I think I've got evidence that this state begins to diminish and become transformed into something healthy rather than stay in an injurious state.

There is another rather important thing about realizing a pattern: I remember hearing an analyst—quite a senior analyst—once saying, "If you see greed, or you see envy, just go for it." I am absolutely certain that that is mistaken because, again, I think, inside the individual feels that the analyst or therapist has been hooked in and smiles in triumph inwardly. It stimulates godlikeness, and the state stays the same. It is quite important, this, because I think that sadly it is quite possible to go through a long analysis where you stay jelly-like, ingest the type of ethos of the analyst and the interpretations and this and that, but with no creative act occurring, and internalization only happens through such an act. Going back to what I said about conscience, that is why it is significant when that woman said, "But this is mad"—then something can begin to act inside, and if it is possible to see these different processes at work—and it *is* possible to see them—the greed where things are all swallowed in a great implosive act, the envy where the good qualities are got rid of—it is possible to see these things and to realize that the person is very much under the dominance of them and if they are interpreted, then this begins to—I don't want to use the word disappear, because actually if there is a healthy developmental functioning those things will be transformed and they'll become, as it were, assets to the personality rather than the opposite.

There are many other examples, but a very common one is when a person disappears as soon as he is out of sight—that people only exist while within the perceptual field. When you are in that state, there are no internal images, and it is important to have this principle in mind—the patient leaves the consulting-room, and you have totally disappeared. Emotionally, you no longer exist. It is a disaster from which they don't recover, really. The "liquifiers" and "petrifiers" have to be understood and interpreted, and when this is done, the inner mind is able to begin to create those internal images which guarantee object constancy.

> *Floor:* I am interested in your thoughts about forgiveness—self-forgiveness—because I am thinking about this concept of the jelly and myself tying it in with a kind of a fear and the need to keep things rigid because of forgiveness coming from within. You were talking yesterday about conscience and about change coming, I think you were saying this, from within the client or patient rather than being given, and you even touched on this a bit today about imprinting rather than really digesting. So I just wondered what your thoughts were about that. I mean, there were some other things, but that will do for the moment, I think.

One of the problems of this whole situation is the very strong tendency within this system: "Yes, I am a rotten bastard, I am hopeless, I am useless, I am a sour bitch, I am no good", that is tremendously strong. When the situation starts to change and there begins to be a different view, perhaps I am not just a "worm" or "filthy insect", then the person can start to forgive themselves. I think that—and I come to this when I touch on the question of perversion—there is a way of speaking that is very current within psychoanalytic discourse that this behaviour is perverse, as if that is an absolute, you see, but the whole meaning of something that is perverse is that somewhere or other there is a right path, that somehow the person has got into this perverse one. What I am trying to get at is the difference between seeing behaviour as purely destructive or self-destructive as opposed to behaviour that is destructive but whose intent was good but, because of the interference of the intensifiers, has become perverted into something destructive. For instance, if someone is operating within this narcissistic system, he may indulge in some type of perverse or cruel behaviour, but it is quite often possible to see that something else is being attempted that's gone wrong. Looked at this way, the person can forgive himself. I think one of the most useful and valuable explanatory ways of thinking is Bion's idea that when something frustrating or painful occurs, the person either evades it or modifies it. One can see that in the evasion what someone is trying to get at and really trying to do, but because they have been caught in this system, it has gone wrong. To put it another way: if conscience is operating and it is *able* to operate and someone responds to it, there is always this very dangerous moment where the person does start to respond to conscience, and they then feel very bad about things in the past, which can lead to suicide, but, on the other hand, they may also reach a point where they can begin to forgive themselves.

> *Floor:* Yes, that was just the other little bit, I remembered it now as you have been talking. It had to do with shame, because you talked quite a lot about guilt yesterday, and I was thinking how shame interferes with that. I am afraid I am ignorant about Bion, but did he talk about shame?

I am not sure, but I tend to look at it his way. I think shame is the emotional register of an inner state that is in an awful mess, whereas guilt is focused on the actions that produce it. The individual in the gelatinous state has shame about being in that state and, being shameful, tries to hide it.

> *Floor:* Shame being something to do with one's being, something you feel about who you are, rather than something you have done or thought?

Yes. I'd just like to be a bit careful about the word "feel", in that I think it is one of the differences between, say, someone who is normal neurotic and someone who is psychotic. My grasp is that in some ways when you get someone who is psychotic, they almost *know* about this state—the jelly-like state—and that they are all broken up and in a mess and they actually speak it. The neurotic person knows that it is there, but they hide it more. The shame is what one might call the subjective emotional register that things are in a mess. It is a bit like when you go to somebody's house unexpectedly and they open the door and they say, "I'm terribly sorry, the whole house is in a total mess", and they are sort of ashamed about it. It is like that inside. Things are in a mess. I think that is what shame is to do with. It will then relate to particular actions which are *because* of that state inside: when things are in an appalling mess inside, we can't look inwards so instead focus totally on the outside. When you hear people saying that someone is not at all psychologically minded or they have got no inner understanding, it may be a way of indicating that it is too much of a mess inside.

> *Floor:* I have been wondering since yesterday if in fact we don't at first intuit or give shape to or make in some kind of way or think through the idea of the absolute in dream. There is something about that, you know, you have talked in the last couple of days and I am well aware that one cannot get at the absolute, the infinite, etc., through total ratiocination. For me, there is something about what we can get from the dream which might help us in that process, or if in fact it can be done. I am sorry if I have introduced a new element, but *mea culpa*!

No, no, I am glad you have, but I also want a moment or two to think. Yes, I think probably dreams might give one some access to it. When someone is totally under the dominance of this situation, there is—certainly the people we meet in the consulting-room—there is something thrusting to try to get away from that, and that's *why* they are in the consulting-room. I think that does relate to the dream life, because I think a dream is essentially a creation and, as you know, Bion thought that psychotic patients didn't seem to dream as much. I think there is that insight of his, that when this sort of state is very dominant what happens is that someone acts, and so as soon as the acting begins to be represented in a dream, it does mean that there is a sort of creative force. I'd almost put it, I think, that the very fact of dreaming already has some origin in what I refer to as "the infinite". I'll give an example that happened once with a woman who came to see me shortly after a very severe breakdown. Initially in the sessions all she could do was to refer to different things in the room and say "clock" or "book" or things like this. I had only just qualified at that time, and I remember saying "My heavens! My training hasn't prepared me for anything like this." I had just one instinct, and this instinct was to try to keep in communication with her, and as she gave me these disparate bits, I linked them with my imagination, I made them into a sort of narrative. I didn't know whether I was talking absolute nonsense or not, but I certainly had the thought that if anyone looked at me and her in that consulting-room through a one-way screen, they would carry us both off to Friern Barnet. The point is this: these communicative bits went on for quite a long time, but then one day she had a dream: the dream was of the body of her mother, and she came up and touched the body, and it blew into a thousand bits. I thought that what has been happening in the consulting-room—all those bits—is now in a dream, and it was very significant that subsequent to that communication, she improved a great deal. That is why I think Bion was so right to correct Freud's view that actually the dream is a creative act that begins to synthesize and bring things together, and so it is not quite an answer to your question, but it is, sort of !

> *Floor:* I just want to take up on that, because what I understood by what you said was that it wasn't that the dream had to be invited into the setting in order for it to be brought into you and to take place. I was thinking about this wonderful example you gave about the drunkard, and what I was thinking about that example was that the problem with having an insight like "I could get better" is that before it takes place, you have no idea that you are capable of such a thought, and when it *has* taken place, you can recognize it somewhere either as a gift, but you can see how it could become internalized. It could become a source of strength, which it clearly was in that person. It seems to me that it is a bit tragic that an insight like that can take place outside the hospital on a bench, if you like, faced with these two options of death on

the one hand or throwing the bottle through the window on the other, and they can be very difficult to allow to happen in the consulting-room.

I think that is one of the reasons why if a well-minded philanthropist had come along and found him on that bench and put his arm around him, that moment wouldn't have happened.

> *Floor:* Well, that is what I mean, yes.

You see, it's the way in which the person is present to the other. I'll deal with this more in the meditation on "God and the Worm". It is not only what the analyst or the other person says; I can think of a woman who said, "Your very presence in the room is a demand", or a man who said, "I know I have to please you, and that paralyses me." When you hear statements of this sort or suspect that, even if unsaid, they are operating, then every iota of the therapist's psychic attention needs to be upon his own mental attitude: to purge himself of all godlikeness, so that he becomes a presence of support; only then is there a chance of any internal movement, change, dream, functioning of conscience, and so on. I think this paralysing presence is a lot more common than we realize.

I have, of course got a whole lot of material and I think it is terribly important that you should hear every word of it, but I think it is far more important that we get some sort of understanding, and if some things don't get said that doesn't matter. If one or two people would like to ask some questions to start with, now is your chance.

> *Floor:* It is for clarification on the pattern of sanity, and are we in fact saying that it underlies all manifestations of madness, including those that might have an organic base. It was to do with the idea that psychiatry had colonized psychoanalysis, and you were talking about how this is the spirit: that we weren't asking the question, what is the spirit underlying these states of mind, and I am just wanting to know whether you are saying that even those states of mind that have an organic base could be approached in this way.

There are obviously some organic conditions that don't fit this schema very well, and one thing that you need always to remember: Bertrand Russell said that if you take any theory and you run it absolutely to its logical conclusion, you end in madness. That applies to what I am telling you too, and that's number one.

But the other thing is that you don't get a human psychology until you get the emotional response, and of course it is very difficult because the two are so closely interrelated. One might say, for instance, about any of the big events in life—birth, adolescence, death—these are the things that happen, and, of course, one would like to say, "Well, these are the things that happen to the body, as it were, and then there is an emotional response to these", but it's not actually the correct way of speaking, because the two are interlinked. Just coming back on the sort of language we do manage, there is the emotional response to situations, to organic happenings, and this system will affect that organic happening enormously. For instance, it is quite often said that depression is caused by a neuronal imbalance in the brain; there are quite a lot of studies to that effect. I don't think it is the correct way of thinking because people get depressed and they have an emotional way of reacting to things in a depressed way as a result of all sorts of things, of which some organic imbalance might be *one*, but it is only one, and the idea that some researchers come along and say, "*This* is what causes depression" is not right. Depression is a result on the emotional register of something that is going on that is not right and that is handicapping to the person; I think this is quite important. I think depression is also quite often the emotional register of something that is handicapping the person which they do not know about, or, more accurately, that they are not aware of. There is, actually, knowledge but not awareness. To give a simple example, a woman came to see me who was an interior decorator, and whenever she was speaking about some sort of project—I think she had been doing some interior decoration of a hotel, and she'd explain how she'd re-sited the stairway or something—then she'd say things like, "Not that it was all that good, really" and other similar pejorative comments. I pointed these out to her, and I then elaborated it a bit further and said that it was like a figure inside that whenever she did something, it says, "Oh, that's not much good, you know." She came because she was very depressed, but subsequent to that session the depression had lifted quite considerably, and I think it was because she had become aware of the thing that was happening—the dysfunctional thing. I'm trying to get at the fact that an explanation on the line of, "Ah, it's because of this organic thing, therefore the person is now schizophrenic" is not right, any more than it is right *because* this person had a mother who was very negligent, *therefore* it's that. It may be, and it may be part of the traumatizing factor, but you can't argue it as closely as that; that's why I find that there is a *pattern* of events, an interacting pattern, rather than a direct correspondence where A causes B. Having said that, of course there are organic conditions—epilepsy and so on—but there is a painter I know quite well whom I saw the other day, and he's gone almost totally blind, he's got just a tiny bit of sight in one eye. You would sort of predict that for a painter that would be the ultimate disaster and that he would be exceedingly depressed and disgruntled, but I have never been able to detect the slightest hint of it, so it depends on how people respond to these events. It is not the event itself, but the emotional response to it.

> *Floor:* I would like to think a bit more of the example that you gave of the woman who came to you complaining that the therapy and analysis hasn't helped because she couldn't communicate with anybody and then came back about the gynaecologist. You had an emotional reaction when she said, "I have found finally somebody with whom to communicate." Your emotional reaction was of being irritated, annoyed, etc., and then *you* decided not to talk about it but to somehow move on to another level of saying, "Well, since yesterday's session you have been able to communicate with somebody." Now, I would like to think a bit more about that. I am aware that you mentioned the fact that if you had said, "Oh, you are attacking therapy and the work we have done", she would have hooked on to that and sort of got you going on that, but I am also interested to think that that type of interpretation that you gave her may sound like a leap—if I put myself in the shoes of the patient—a leap. I would like to think a bit more whether there could be another kind of talking to her which would have taken into account your emotional reaction, which I am sure you must have digested and processed, and then *you* decided to talk about whatever you talked to her about.

Yes, I would just like to say that in me it wasn't quite as cognitive as you are putting it. I think that this is quite important in that I felt the initial irritation and that when the irritation subsided, I saw clearly that a positive statement was being made. Some clinicians with whom I have discussed this example have said, "No, no, you should actually point out the fact of the provocative nature of the comment." I don't agree with that, and the reason I don't agree with it is this: when someone is in a very disturbed state, as she was, there is a terrifically powerful negative force inside telling her that she is useless, she is hopeless, she doesn't deserve to be alive, and I think that any type of reference to that just reinforces. Therefore I think that one's actual job in that situation is to process it and actually pick up the positive statement that was being made. Just technically—I can't remember whether it happened with her or not—at a very much later stage, in a different type of context and atmosphere, I think it would then be possible to make some comment about the provocative way in which the person sometimes communicates, but certainly not when it is in full flight like that, and I feel as certain as I can be about that, really. I think if one goes back to the point I am getting at which is that she is making a negative statement to me, but actually it is telling one what a powerful negativity there is inside *her* that is attacking *her* the whole time; if you as an outsider touch on it, even by saying, "Listen, you know, this statement you are making is quite negative and I think the reason you are saying it is . . .", it's no good because all the person hears is "This statement is very negative"—they don't hear the sentence on either side of it. When someone is in this state, there is what I call a "zoom-lens effect", and it just homes in on the bit of the negativity that is there; therefore I feel as certain as I can be that my response to her then was the correct one. I can give you many instances where I did the opposite and I am absolutely certain it was a mistake.

> *Floor:* I was thinking that it could be a kind of relief that someone would take appropriate matters to a gynaecologist rather than to a therapist, because it seems she was able to do that.

Yes, yes, she could begin to realize that there is a wider world than me, you know.

Floor: Yes, I have been worrying at this in my mind ever since I had a go at reading your book, *Emotion and Spirit*; yesterday you talked about the survival instinct being a sort of physical thing probably linked with your idea of a primitive religion, and I kept being bothered and saying "But what about, in more advanced societies, an instinct for psychic survival." There is the terror, I mean, you haven't as yet referred to childhood experiences and I am terribly impressed by that, but what we grow up with in the way of terrors of extinction, or not being seen, or being devalued, presumably is part of the jelly, and the crust that we form is part of psychic survival we *believe*. I was wondering about a middle position where people try, I agree with you that therapy is about trying to come out from there, but people try to take up middle positions where they find something vaguely firm inside themselves, bring it out, introduce it to the outside world, and depend terribly on what kind of reception that gets. In therapy that is ok because if you get a reasonable therapist, they are supposed to be giving you a reasonable reception. If you are not—I mean, I am a marital psychotherapist, and I know that if you manage to make a reasonable marriage, for example, a lot of that early terror can be modified through the experience of negotiating a reasonable marriage. However, I am really asking about this middle position of an instinct. Would you agree that there might be an instinct for psychic self-protection?

Well, look, I think a very important thing which will come out—incidentally, infancy and that is going to come out in this talk. This system that I was pointing out is the best system that the person has been able to manage with, and I think that it is very important that it doesn't get condemned. I certainly think that there is a place within where it is necessary to reach a point where the patient understands and you understand with them that they actually *needed* this and that, as it were, in this sort of a system where there has often been a very savage God, but it is sometimes represented in some other figure, that savage though it has been, it has, in a sense, looked after them although it has had bad consequences. I think quite a lot of the talk about the internal Mafia and the internal malefactors and internal saboteurs and so on fails to take account of the fact that these figures looked after the person, and it was the best they could manage with; in a way, when someone comes for treatment, they are saying, "Look, it has managed me quite well, but I need something else because it is crippling me in other ways."

Floor: Could that be part of the forgiveness of the self?

Yes, I think so, yes I do, I certainly think so, and I think that is terribly important, actually.

MEDITATION FOUR

Emotional action and strengthening of the ego

It is not possible to discuss this whole matter without talking about emotions, because the central thing—our central material, as it were—are the emotions, and I think it is rather important to try to get some grasp of them. To start with, emotions are not the same as feelings. I think a lot of confusion arises because people talk about feelings and emotions synonymously. Emotions are unseen activities. Love, for instance, or hate—both or either of these are unseen. You may see all sorts of signs of them, but they are activities; but you will *feel* them if you walk into a room and someone who is exceedingly hateful and hostile is there—you will feel that, most likely. When you try to describe it—say, someone says, "Why do you dislike that person so much?" and you say, "Oh, well, you know, when I arrived he didn't open the door and he turned the other way, or he scowled when I was talking to him." These are all attempts, but they are not actually quite the reason. It is because the emotion itself is like an unseen action that can be registered in the feelings.

Feelings can, I think, be divided up crudely into two sorts. If you are under the dominance of this sort of narcissistic constellation, your feelings all tend to register how things affect *you*.

Whereas there is another way in which feelings operate, and this is when they go out and register the contours of the person that you are speaking to. I remember once going to a sculpture exhibition, and, unusually, there was a notice saying "Please Feel the Statues", which is the opposite of what you normally expect—so, in fact, you could *feel* these statues. That is one sort of a feeling, but there is the other, which is basically how I am affected. So if you take it like the example I gave when I was irritated when that woman said that, that is a feeling being processed through that narcissistic system. What I actually then said to her, those were then feelings processed through the other side.

Take a bee stinging the photographer's thumb, and the photographer has managed to take the photograph at that precise moment. That is quite an interesting symbol in a way—the photographer no doubt suffered the pain of the bee sting, but he also thought that it was interesting enough to bear that and to photograph it. If he had been totally dominated by avoiding the sting, then we wouldn't have that photograph.

As it is so common within psychoanalytic discourse, you have probably heard of a phrase called "projective identification". What it means is when something inside the self is hated and expelled. Though that is not quite the right way of describing it, because the expulsion *is* the hatred—primitive hatred *is* the expulsion. If you actually feel yourself hating, then you are at a higher level of operation, and that is why I said I thought that the word paranoia probably isn't all that good. When you are paranoid in relation to someone, it is because there is something hated inside yourself that you have expelled. I might say, you haven't just expelled it like that: it is an expulsion that takes place through noting an equivalence—you notice a hated element in the other person, and it is then possible to transmit the hated element inside yourself into the equivalent location in the other person. That is what is meant by "projective identification". One of the reasons I put stress on the human desire for freedom is that when there is an element inside the personality, inside yourself, which you hate, why do you hate it? You hate it because it restricts your freedom. So if you have omnipotence inside you, greed, envy, it handicaps your freedom, and that is why it is hated. This is where Bion's notion comes in

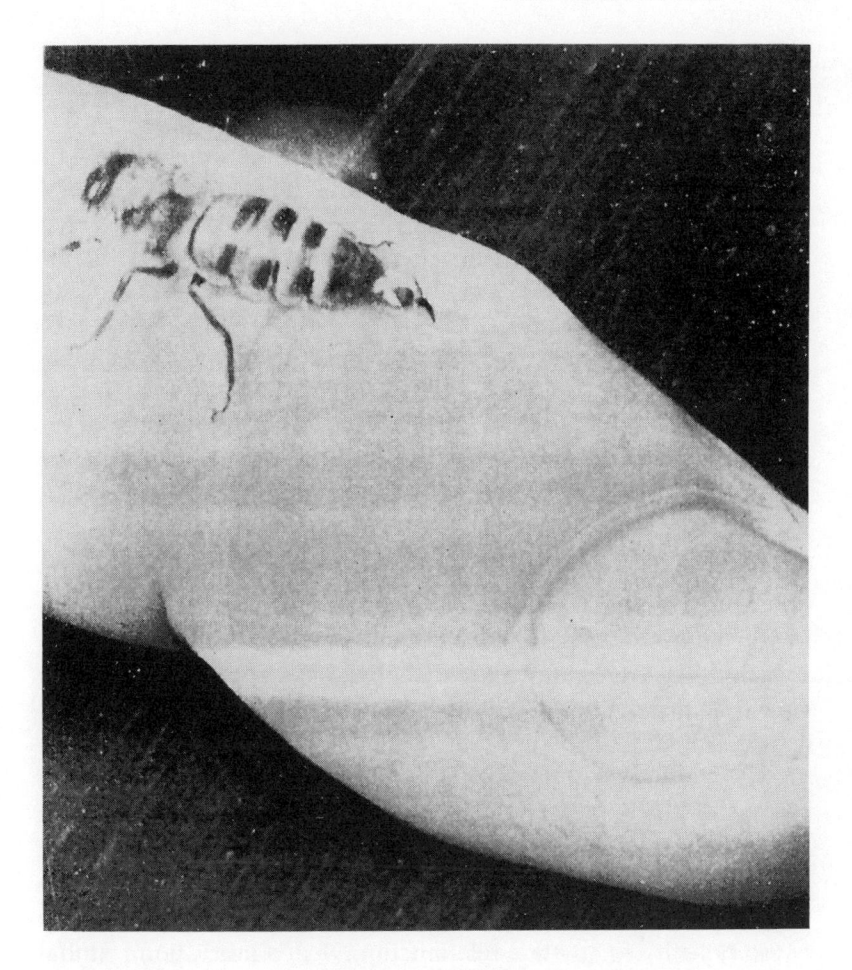

about how you deal with something: either you try to modify it, or you can't face the pain so you get rid of it. I use the word "hatred" because it comes across to me as a word that most of us understand and the man in the street understands, and it is also that the violence of the emotion comes across. I am very struck by the amount of anodyne language that gets used within psychoanalytic discourse. You very often hear someone say, "Oh, and he denied it"; that is very wishy-washy, but if you say "They *hate* it", then you get some sense of what is going on in the personality. The point is that you can say that there is good intent there, that the person is wanting to be free of something that is actually clogging them up, but one of the paradoxes is that the very hatred of it in fact impoverishes the personality, because the personality requires all that you have got inside—the shadow side and the other side—you need it all. So, for instance, if you get rid of things in that way, you can't then face difficult emotional situations. I wrote a paper once on the response aroused by the psychopath. If you are unfortunate enough to encounter someone who is psychopathic, it requires enormous strength and resolve and resolution inside yourself to stand up to that; but if, for instance, you have some greed in you which you hate and have got rid of, you would never be able to stand up to the psychopath, and that is just one example.

I am saying all that just as an introduction, because that's all quite familiar within analytic discourse, except this business about freedom. It is important to realize *why* it is that someone wants to get rid of it. It is also one of the reasons why the person is nearly always stuck to the person about whom they are paranoid—because there is actually part of themselves there that they need. Emotions are also creative, and that is why I stressed that thing about the infinite or the absolute. The emotions have the power to create. It is difficult to conceptualize that the response is created. We tend to think that if the response is created, then it is not free on the part of the responder, but that is not true. It is totally different from manipulation, but if there is a creative emotional activity, it can produce a good response. We often think of creativity in terms of art, music, and so on, but actually a much more basic creativity is the capacity to create a relationship. This is much more fundamental and essential. It is, I think, one of the reasons why autism, which is often described as the inability of the infant to make a relationship, means that there is an elemental failure in the capacity to create, because a relationship is something that is created. There is an example of this in my book on narcissism. It is an example that Graham Greene gives in one of his autobiographical books about the literary critic Herbert Read:

> Certainly my meeting with Herbert Read was an important event in my life. He was the most gentle man I have ever known, but it was a gentleness which had been tested in the worst experiences of his generation. The young officer, who

gained the Military Cross and a DSO in action on the Western Front, had carried with him, to all that mud and death, Robert Bridge's anthology *The Spirit of Man*, Plato's *Republic*, and *Don Quixote*. Nothing had changed in him. It was the same man twenty years later who could come into a room full of people and you wouldn't notice his coming. You noticed only that the whole atmosphere of a discussion had quietly altered, that even the relations of one guest with another had changed. No one any longer would be talking for effect and when you looked round for an explanation there he was—complete honesty born of complete experience had entered the room and taken a chair. [Greene, 1980, p. 39]

That is quite a remarkable passage, and it illustrates what emotions are able to create, so it is quite important in terms of the therapeutic situation. We often talk about what patients put into the analyst and the anger they stir up in the analyst and so on. All of this is true, though I'd never ever use a phrase like "putting into". But what if the analyst suddenly has an insight and an understanding: that might also have been generated from a creative urge in the patient, but we do not hear of that very much. The negativity, the worm-like state, courses through the veins of analytic societies like a poisonous injection. Whenever there is a creative thought, it comes as a result of a benign emotional creativity that is at work.

Now I want to come to how this relates to babies and infants. It is much easier to describe the bad things that are done than the absence of good things. For instance, I know there is a group in the Tavistock who put a lot of stress on mothers who project stuff that belongs to them into the babies, and so the baby becomes the carrier of projections, and I am sure that is true. I think it is again quite important to see how the infant conjures up to the mother an image of something that she hates, and which she then expels into the infant. I don't think, however, that this is primary. The primary deficit is the mother's failure to contemplate her baby—and I use the word "contemplation" rather than Bion's "reverie" or even Freud's "free-floating attention". I use that word because it conjures up a more active, related-to-the-object sense. To try to understand what I mean by contemplation—and it's part of what I am trying to say about a spirituality that is relevant to the interrelation between people—the seers of the Upanishads were contemplatives. They started through meditation, and they then moved into a contemplative act where they had an understanding of themselves and the universe as a single unity, and they then also realized the implications of what this meant for their own way of living. In the Christian tradition there have always been nuns and monks whose whole vocational dedication has been to attempt to achieve contemplation, and again it is contemplating the infinite, the absolute. I personally think that in all the great religious traditions the founders had a lot of primitive and unspiritual stuff mixed in, and the work of the mystics and contemplatives was to purify and understand. What I am getting at is this. It seems to me that *the* place where contemplation is needed is not in monasteries or convents or in hermitages or whatever, but, rather, the place where contemplation is needed is by the mother with her baby. This means a realization of this particular infant, and a contemplative act brings this to life. I think Melanie Klein was trying to get at something like this when she talked about the bad breast, but if you think about it, I am pretty certain that when you get people who are full of the most awful internal objects, real monsters inside them, it is their way of representing an *absence*, because there is no way within the human equipment to produce an image of an *absence*. I remember a philosopher telling me once that he sometimes woke in the middle of the night and used to try to think of the universe and the fact that the universe must somehow be limited. It is a very facile picture, but he said, "I sometimes wake in the middle of the night and imagine myself going right to the end of the universe, and at the end of the universe there is a high wall, and I climb the wall, and there is *nothing* on the other side, *nothing*, but you always imagine something shadowy something, you can't actually imagine nothing. It is not possible." So also, if there is the absence of something, the only way the human psyche can represent an absence is by some sort of savage monster in one form or another. The savage monster may be in imagery, but at a more primitive level the person will not have in them an image of a monster but will *act* a monster, *be* a monster. That is the only way an absence can be represented. I think this is important too when we hear about the sexual abuse of children, which I am sure needs attention. If, when there has been sexual abuse, you ask yourself, "Look—what's actually absent here, why has this happened?", that is usually far more important, because the physical act of the abuse, horrifying though it may be, is probably nothing like as bad as what is absent.

The other thing that is quite important is the realization of how important that capacity for contemplation in the mother is. It does not *have* to be the mother— contemplation of her child is not necessarily accompanied by good nurture all the time. Obviously the ideal is for the infant to be well nurtured and cared for. Some people have had an appalling upbringing, but somehow they manage very well; I think a contemplative act that is transmitted can be something that provides the child with an inner sense of wellbeing. It may give the child something crucially important within when on the surface it may look as if the rest of their life, or their caring, has been very poor. I think this is directly related to what I have been talking about: it is the contemplation of the infinite, but in this particular form, in the infant.

Over the years I have had several patients who have been silent for long periods, and I have noticed two things: (1) that in a contemplative silence I have had new psychological understandings, and (2) that such patients have subsequently been able to make a closer relationship than has been possible before. I think these two have been connected: my own act of contemplation and the increased capacity for emotional closeness.

The contemplative act takes the person beyond the infant and yet is like a healing balm that reaches deep inside it, endowing the structure with new life. It is as if the contemplative act is having a moment of x-ray where you can see the inner structure.

I think contemplation of this sort is a *work*, but it is very important to realize that it is not a conscious or anxious work, but it is a work in the same way as you talk about mourning being a work. I remember when seeing one such silent patient I was conscious that it was a bigger emotional effort—though that isn't the right word— I know it pulled more out of me emotionally than seeing anyone else. It is difficult exactly to explain why that is, but I think the need to somehow contemplate and to draw upon certain experiences that I knew about him and say the odd things—and quite an important thing, this, because I don't know how many of you have had silent patients—it is very easy to speak in such a way as if you are beginning to say "I think you are being silent because of such and such", i.e. you shouldn't be silent. It is the same old story, you see.

I was very struck by an article in the *Infant Observation Journal* by Didier Houzel, where he gives remarkable instances of where autistic infants, or young autistic children, were being healed of their condition through the receptive attention of the therapist. However, the therapist acted very much like someone doing Infant Observation: saying nothing and just watching. He gives a very illustrative example where one of his team went one day to a house, and the mother was bathing the baby; the observer sat in the bathroom on a stool, watching, and the water in the bath almost came right over the baby's head, and just at that moment the mother went out. He was left observing this and was in enormous anxiety that the baby's head would just plunge under the water, and he had all sorts of feelings about the mother—how a mother can do this, and so on—but the therapist managed to hold this and contain it. The next time the therapist came back, the child was bright and communicative in a way that it hadn't been before. So again there seemed to be a link between the therapist's contemplative act and the infant's ability to communicate. One is always in danger of romanticizing something, and I am always rather fearful that when I say that an inner act of generosity or love builds up the strength of the ego, it will be misunderstood, and in the same way what I am saying about contemplation also could be very easily misunderstood. What I am trying to get at is that emotions, apart from what we all know about projective identification, have this creative function.

Floor: Please, Neville, would you say a few more words about what you thought was happening in that bathroom?

Let's just put it in this way: when the mother went out of the bathroom, it was an act of hate, and the therapist who stayed in the bathroom was able to receive it and process it.

Floor: And if he had to put his hands into the bath-water and lifted out the baby's head to save it from drowning, would that have made any difference?

I'm not sure that it would, actually. Emotions are very frequently associated with actions, so it would depend on when he acted in that way and took the baby's head out of the water—whether in the moment of doing it there had been some emotional thing inside him that said, "Bloody mother!" or some internal correlate of that, then I think there would have been no healing. Had he done it and managed to maintain a receptivity to the hatred, then I think it would have been all right.

> *Floor:* The baby must have seen the observer. There must have been something.

I don't think there is any doubt about that. I have read most of the writings of Isaiah Berlin, the historian of ideas. He is particularly interested in those philosophers and thinkers who swam against the current. In fact, the title of one of his books is *Against the Current*, and it is about those people who stood up against the common over-arching view. One of the philosophers that he is particularly interested in is Giovanni Battista Vico, who was quite unknown in his day—in the seventeenth century, in Naples. In a way it is quite a simple thing: Vico said, "There is a way of knowing that is not just through the senses", but rather there is a way of knowing that is, I think, what you are talking about. There was some knowing in the baby. Isaiah Berlin said, talking about Vico:

> This way of knowing is a species of its own. It is knowing founded on memory or imagination. It is not analysable except in terms of itself, nor can it be identified save by examples. . . . This is the sort of knowing which participants in an activity claim to possess as against mere observers: the knowledge of the actors as against that of the audience, of the 'inside' story as opposed to that obtained from some 'outside' vantage point; knowledge by 'direct acquaintance' with my inner states or by sympathetic insight into those of others. . . .The knowledge that is involved when a work of the imagination or social diagnosis or a work of criticism or scholarship or history is described *not* as correct or incorrect, skilful or inept, a success or a failure, *BUT* as profound or shallow, realistic or unrealistic, perceptive or stupid, alive or dead. [Berlin & Hardy, 1979]

Berlin is saying that there is a special form of knowledge of this sort, and I think that this is the sort of thing that baby received from that person sitting there.

Floor: It strikes me that the observer was also functioning like the father, and that I think the whole triad is interesting in that the mother knew that the observer was there. I feel that the mother was looking for the father to act and to be able to contain her hatred, and also, possibly, testing the observer out to see if the observer was going to be a critical mother of *her* as a mother, but it seems to me that the baby would have picked up from the mother that the mother was leaving the baby with the father. The father's capacity, for me, to function as an other to the mother and to contain the mother's hatred is part of the function of the father at these sorts of times.

Yes, I think that, but again one could look at it in this other way. Was it a destructive act on the part of the mother, or not? Actually, as it turns out, it wasn't. Had the observer got in an agitated state, then it would have been.

Floor: But it isn't destructive to use the father for that function.

No, no, I'm not sure that it quite matters whether it was the father or . . .

Floor: No, another.

. . . another, who the observer was.

Floor: That was why I thought the observer could also be the mother's mother—the mother's uncritical mother who could process her own hatred.

I prefer to think of it more in this way: that the event happened. We don't know what would have happened if the mother's mother had been there, or the mother's husband had been there—the result might have been different. One just doesn't know, you see.

Floor: I was thinking more of an internal mother rather than a real mother.

Ah, yes, but I think that situation wasn't one in which an internal mother had been functioning properly, in the mother because that sort of act doesn't have to occur if that had been the case.

Floor: I was going to say that it suddenly seemed to be someone that the mother put her trust in, that the other person was someone the mother trusted, one assumes, and the baby consequently felt, perhaps.

Yes, I think that is true, and that is why I stress the notion of emotions and actions, because when she trusts, that is an action on the part of the mother. I think it is terribly important to distinguish between ordinary mobile activity and emotional actions. Trust is an emotional act and has a creative effect, so you can certainly think of it that way, that the mother trusted this therapist/observer.

Floor: It may be something to do with the quality of attention that the observer maintained, which in some way held and allowed that to happen safely?

Oh, yes, I am sure of that. Didier Houzel actually explains in his article that he had a team of people who did this therapeutic work, and they came back and had seminars, where it was discussed in an attempt to understand what was happening. He says in that article that one of the biggest difficulties was parents who would ask for this therapeutic help and then found it difficult to think that something was actually going on, because they expected the therapist to be directive and doing visible practical things, and instead the person just came in, sat, and observed. There were two or three cases where the parent said: "Oh, no, we are going to take this to a decent paediatrician in Paris."

Floor: But you just said "just observed", and surely that is the point, it *isn't* just observing.

No, no, you are quite right. The observation is a contemplative act, which is enormously fruitful.

Floor: But I mean there is a quality that is a contemplative thing in its own right.

Oh, absolutely, yes, it is.

Floor: An action of love, it makes the baby feel alive.

I think so. I went recently to Ruskin's house overlooking Coniston Water, and there was a quote there from him, where he says, "Of the millions of people who talk only a few thousand think and of the few thousand who think only a very rare few observe." I think it was that sort of observation.

> *Floor:* Just a last word about this, because I feel as if we have been struggling towards the idea of a couple, that somewhere the containing of this baby happened because of something that went on between a couple. That's something that hasn't come up a lot so far, the function of how you can't attend unless you are attended to, or it is very hard—that would be beyond, wouldn't it.

Yes, it's an instance of the capacity of the emotions to create. It is a creative interaction, and it is that strange way in which when the creative function comes into the ascendant, things are suddenly all seen differently.

> *Floor:* Your lecture reminds me of a patient, and I know very well what you were saying about this kind of thing. I have been looking for the word—contemplation. I was very creative in a long phase of silence and had a lot of ideas about this patient and his history and his kind of being as a very poor intellectual, and I was very content with it and was very creative also, and I thought, "The silence is OK", but he said he was empty. So my question is, in a kind of projective identification, did I take his creativity and be very active while he was empty? Can this contemplation also work in this sense?

Oh, yes, I certainly think that, and it is that subtle type of realization that can occur, isn't it, that it is necessary to be silent. Say, with a patient who is silent for three months, you are confronted with the question of when to speak or when not to speak, or, "Would it be better not to say anything in this session." There is nothing to trust, but the fact of what you do and whether you do this or that is significant, and it is absolutely definite. I always think it is one of the great dilemmas about supervision, for instance, that it is not something that you can legislate for. That moment where you realize and you think, "Heavens, I'll draw back from saying anything about this", or there is a slight prompt and you realize that it is better to say nothing—those things must be terribly relevant. I can think of a patient who would always rather prompt one to say something, and then I noticed that if I didn't and just held back and stayed quiet, then *he* would come out with a creative thought. Quite what it is that leads one to realize that, from what I was saying before—it's part of the creative process that is going on. It is always going on, there is the expelling or projective thing prompting me perhaps to speak or say something, but there is another that is actually getting through somewhere else, and you think, "Hold off, Neville, just be quiet."

> *Floor:* We talk very often about containment, and we answer work on containment. In the example you gave, you really then talked about the observers containing the mother's hatred and processing it. Maybe we keep these two actions of containment and reverie, or contemplation, too separate, because it seemed to me that she was digesting the hatred but she was also contemplating with love this baby, and so it is the action of the love as well as the taking in of the hatred and digesting it. I thought that may be linked to your example about what you did with the patient who went to the gynaecologist. That you both digested the anger, but you also contemplated something good and loving in her seeking new connections. So maybe the two should be more brought together.

Well, I do think that is right, and that is why I said about the word reverie that I don't think the word reverie and containment is quite sufficient really.

> *Floor:* Quite. The action of digesting the hatred or the distress and the loving investment with life in the baby.

Yes. I think there's a difference between reverie and a loving act or a contemplative act, because in the latter the actual contours of the baby are seen. That is why I gave the example of the statue: you actually then *feel* the contours of the statue as opposed to feeling a bee-sting. When you are under the dominance of that other constellation, then you are just feeling the way you are affected or the way you are hurt or wounded etc., so it *blocks* the act of contemplation.

Floor: Because we have talked about containment, but maybe it is the other in addition . . .

Yes, I think so. I do think that.

Floor: I am just groping towards something, and that thing is the difference that you have been talking about between personality and the absolute; it is something to do with that surrender, that willingness, not to react from personality, but to open up to something that is beyond that personality self, and which can then inform your action and prompt. I think what Jonathan talked about, "a gift", that something new can come into that situation which is beyond that limited personality self which reacts with greed, envy, jealousy, hatred, annoyance, and so on—a willingness to kind of open up those boundaries to some extent and sit for a moment in not knowing and maybe reach to goodwill. I'm not putting it very well, but it is a distinction, and I think it is something that I differed from you in thinking of the absolute as *not* part of the personality actually, that it is a willingness to open up those boundaries of the personality self, which then enables a connection, an encounter, with the absolute, which is actually transforming and creative; it is transforming through the creativity inherent in that situation.

I don't agree with that. I think that what is referred to as the infinite, or Bion referred to as O or the absolute—it is not even right to say it's *in* the personality. You can't separate in your mind this wooden table from its shape. It always has to be in a shape. That's not a very good example, but the infinite, the absolute, reality, is in many forms. It is not outside it. The greater, the infinite is not outside it. The mystery is how that can be. Spinoza said, "There is just one substance, that is all there is, one reality"—but then he has the problem of describing how you get diversity, and then he says "There are different modes", but it doesn't exactly answer it. In religion it has always been recognized that this is a mystery. Even within the Judaeo–Christian system, where I think the way it has been formulated is perhaps not the most helpful, there is the idea of God as a being totally perfect in himself, so then why create? All the great theologians have said that is a mystery. You can't grasp it.

EMOTIONAL ACTION

The other way, the Eastern way of looking at it, is that all reality that we see is that there is reality—being in its many manifestations—but it's beyond the mind to grasp how it can be manifested in different ways if it's one. The mind just can't quite grasp it. Parmenides wasn't crackers, he was trying to grasp it. But the real significance, the real emotional significance for us is that we are in it—so there is this dual constitution of the personality.

To put it another way, when you think of the debate that goes on about priority, for instance, in intellectual and academic circles: if there is a thought that is really constructive and helpful to human beings, why is it so important that it was first thought by Freud or by Bion or by Einstein? Or if I have a thought, why should I actually worry if someone says to me, "So and so pinched your thought." It is very odd that it should be a worry. If you really think about it, why should it matter to me? People get frightfully hot under the collar: "This was Freud's idea." Why does it really matter? I admire those beautiful statues in mediaeval cathedrals whose sculptors are frequently anonymous.

MEDITATION FIVE

God and the worm

In my paper called "The True and the False God" (Appendix A), I try to differentiate between God in the way I have been speaking about the absolute, the infinite, and the popular idea of God as a figure who directs us and tells us what to do (visual aid: Intensifiers—see frontispiece). The seers who gave rise to the Upanishads understood what I call the true God is the way. The Chandogya Upanishad is one of the oldest. There is also a type of power of God that is quite different from that. There is a story that most people, certainly of a Christian education, will find familiar:

> He got into the boat followed by his disciples. Without warning a storm broke out over the lake, so violent that the waves were breaking right over the boat but he was asleep. So they went to him and woke him saying, "Save us, Lord, we are going down!" He said to them, "Why are you so frightened, you men of little faith?" And with that he stood up and rebuked the winds and the sea, and all was calm again. The men were astounded and said, "Whatever kind of man is this? Even the winds and the sea obey him."

I want to stress that in all the great religions there is a jewel of great price, but there are also elements that I believe are harmful. It is quite clear to me, for instance, that Jesus said some profound truths, but he also said things that I don't think have been helpful. Very often, when you hear people presenting a patient clinically, they say things like "And so the patient just obliterated it from their mind" or "They just smothered it" or "They sealed it over" or "They got rid of it." One of the things that I think is very important when you hear things like that is to ask, *who* got rid of it, and *who* sealed over, and *what* was it in the personality that did this. It is the God in the personality that gets rid of pain, suffering, guilt, sadness. I remember once making an interpretation that was helpful to someone, and it took me some time to realize that as soon as I said something that was helpful, she had taken the words and invested them with a sort of magical power. All her difficulties—her shyness—were gone forever, so, as it were, Jesus had stood up and rebuked the shyness and a great calm had settled on the Galilee of her mind. You have to ask yourself whenever you hear a clinical presentation, and you hear "such and such was sealed over" etc., what it was in the personality that did it. That's why I come back to the point I made before that there is no significance in pointing out omnipotence in someone *unless* one can show them that this God—and I prefer to call it God because that actually means something to people—this God in the personality gets rid of things, or gets rid of suffering, obliterates what has been said, etc.—particularly pain.

So the question you might ask is, "Where is this God?" It wouldn't be accurate to say that it has been installed in the psychoanalyst, or in the psychotherapist because it is probably installed in both the patient *and* the analyst. The words spoken by the analyst or by the patient can become divinized and receive a divine stamp upon them. A woman said, "Now I understand that I have been trying all my life to protect myself against painful experiences." That sounds quite innocent, and the analyst sits back quite comfortably and doesn't realize that these words she has spoken are invested with godly power, so now she believes that she no longer protects herself in that way because the magic words have been spoken. I am trying to get at the God in the personality that gets rid of things and also in the sort of way that something is said; someone may have already climbed a little way up the mountain, and they believe that they are now at the top of it.

Taking the case of the God condemning: the patient regularly undermines an interpretation, and the analyst says, "I think the reason behind this undermining is envy." But the patient, as I have said, doesn't hear that dispassionately but rather that he is being pronounced evil. It may not be felt as condemnation for evil, but rather that there is an underlying assumption that really he is just a worthless insect, totally devoid of worth, and that is why whenever this God is present in the personality, the other is always present. The significance of this is that you might get the person who comes to you full of a sense of worthlessness, saying to herself, "I am hopeless, and my life is no good, and I am no use" etc. It is a great help if you realize that the God is in there too, nearly always. It is not right to say that the person is feeling that way *because* God is condemning—it is as if there is a bad pair. So what has happened in a statement like that is that the analyst's two statements get congealed into one. The first is, "There is envy in you"; the second is, "You are a rotten, worthless member of society and an insect that deserves to be crushed." The two get congealed into one; it is one of the features that when God speaks, things get congealed, and they don't get separated out. But the same thing can happen when the analyst speaks a sympathetic sentiment, if he is installed as God. So, for instance, when the analyst says, "When I spoke too harshly just now, you felt hurt", the patient felt hurt not because he *felt* hurt, but because it had been pronounced by God that he felt hurt. It is quite important to get that difference. This may sound a little bit exaggerated, but as I have come to think about this and reflect a bit more on it, I very rarely say to a patient, "You are feeling such and such" or even "I *think* you are feeling such and such." The reason is this: if they are feeling it, there is no reason to say it, because feeling is actually part of consciousness. When you say "I feel something", you are saying, "I am conscious of this." So if you say to someone, "You feel upset by such and such", if they are conscious of it, then it's a completely vacuous statement; if they are not conscious of it, it does not exist as a feeling. It may sound a nice point, but it is terribly important, and I think Bion said, and Freud definitely did, quite correctly: "There is no feeling in the unconscious." I am going to make an arrogant bet that 90 per cent of us speak in every session to our patients about how they feel. It is worth thinking about. Part of the trouble is that if the analyst is installed as God, the person feels that, but it is not as a result of their own feeling. They have been told, "That is what you feel", and so they feel it. There is a great need to try to develop psychological understanding. The muddle within the psychotherapeutic and psychoanalytic world is absolutely appalling. To give an example of that business of feeling and consciousness. I think it can't really be realized that actually when someone says "I feel something", they are saying, "I am conscious of it." It first struck me in a rather odd way when a patient said something to me. I can't quite remember what it was, but she told me that her husband had been on a trip to a different city the previous day, and then I referred to this fact, and she said, "I don't feel that's right"—but I *knew* that it was right that she had told me. One of the biggest sources of error within the psychotherapeutic movement is that if the analyst *feels* something, then that must be right, or if the patient *feels* something that must be right. If the feeling is transmitted through this system, it doesn't necessarily correspond to the truth.

Now I want to move on from God and the Worm to the subject of evil (visual aid: Intensifiers—see frontispiece). We can't talk about religion without coming up against evil. I don't think it requires any building-up of evidence to know that there is the most shocking, treacherous behaviour in the world, and one doesn't have to look far in this past century to see it, so it's a real thing. The question is, when we talk about something that is evil in the personality or destructive in the personality, what do we mean? To attempt an answer, I will quote from a Jewish mystical book called *The Zohar*, written by a man called Moses de Leon in the fourteenth century in Spain. It is a book that is written in epigrammatic form, not systematic, rather like Nietsche's *Thus Spake Zarathustra*. I haven't got any direct knowledge of the book, but I have read the distillation of it by Gershom Scholem in his classic book, *Major Trends in Jewish Mysticism*. Scholem says there that the author of the Zohar sees the good as a harmonious whole: "The totality of divine potencies forms a harmonious whole, and as long as each stays in relation to all others, it is sacred and good." I hadn't read that book at the time when I wrote the book on narcissism, but I did say there that narcissism was fundamentally a failure of being in relation—not in relation externally but also internally. The important point there is the idea that anything that is split off from the personality is evil; it is good if it is embraced within the personality. The Zohar's definition of evil, its defining feature, is that it is something split off from the personality. Albert Mason, who is a Kleinian analyst in California, said to me once that he thought that the whole endeavour of the psychoanalytic process was to reclaim spilt-off parts. The interesting thing about that is that if you define it in that way, then if it is in relation to the rest of the personality, it is good.

You see here the danger. If we are installed as God and we talk of greed or envy and jealousy, we are in our nature really talking about entities that are disowned. When I talk about God being installed in the personality, you will think of particular schools of analysts who tend to get into that position. There is also another school of analysts who equally get into that position by allowing the inner critic, the inner savage God, to remain within. On the business of transformation, my wife argues in a paper called "The Survival Function of Primitive Omnipotence" that it is actually of value, but, again, it accumulates value only if it is integrated and becomes part of the personality. I'll come shortly to the question of *how* this gets installed in the personality. The psychological process is understood in such a way that these things can begin to be incorporated. What's greed? If you think of it as something that is disowned and split off from the personality, it is harmful, but if it is incorporated, it is transformed into confidence. It changes in its nature.

The author of *The Zohar* also says that "The metaphysical cause of evil is seen in an act which transforms the category of judgement into an absolute." That is what I have meant when I have said that things get congealed into one, so if you speak about someone's mishandling of something or their greed, it very easily gets congealed into an absolute of the wrong sort—that is, that the person is totally a disaster—and of course once that is the case, the person can't find the sort of resources inside themselves to recover from this. It's very easy (1) for the analyst to get into the condemning position, the God position. But there is also the other one which is a very common situation: (2) where a patient says, "I've just thought of something, but I am a bit afraid of saying it, because I feel that you will disapprove." It is not uncommon for someone to say in reply to that, "I wonder *why* you think that I'll disapprove." That is actually another way of saying, "Don't worry, I won't disapprove"—that's actually what it means, and then the person comes forth with a bit of information, whatever that might be. It is quite a problem if that therapy ends up where that person can never say anything if they fear that the therapist is going to disapprove. The therapy hasn't really got very far, and it is very common for that to happen. Actually, the person's *problem* is managing a situation in the face of disapproval, so the answer needs to be much more on the lines of "Well let's say I *do* disapprove of this, what's the difficulty, what's the problem we are struggling with?"—something like that. There are many versions and varieties of that, but it is the case where what I call the analyst, rather than getting into the position of the condemning God, is saying "Don't worry, there is no condemning God around, don't worry"—and of course it is still there, undealt with.

There is an incident in *The Buddha* that I think is quite important, and again I am going to contrast it with a passage from Jesus in the Gospels. This is the incident from the Buddhist scriptures: "Upali who was a follower of Mahavira came to dispute with the Buddha but was convinced by the Buddha's teaching and begged him to accept him as one of his Upasakas (disciples) but the Buddha counselled him not to be in a hurry and to consider it carefully. When he did finally receive him he asked him to continue to respect and support his old religious teachers as he had in the past." The Buddha then says, "Whosoever honours his own religion and condemns other religions, does do indeed through devotion to his own religion thinking 'I will glorify my own religion.' But on the contrary, in so doing he injures his own religion more gravely. So concord is good: Let all listen, and be willing to listen to the doctrines professed by others."

I believe the Buddha had deficits in his teaching, but you can compare it with this statement from the Gospels (Matthew 23): Jesus says, "Alas for you Scribes and Pharisees, you hypocrites, you shut up the kingdom of Heaven in men's faces neither going in yourselves nor allowing others to go in who want to. Alas for you Scribes and Pharisees, you hypocrites, you travel over sea and land to make a single proselyte, and when you have him you make him twice as fit for hell as you are." I have just quoted two verses out of a very long diatribe. I think there is the same danger in psychoanalytic practice, when we talk about the Mafia or the saboteur or the malefactor, if we take that idea that evil comes about because the condemnation leads to the element in the personality being split off and alienated from the family in the personality. The two are interplayed with one another. That's why atheism is frequently a psychological attempt to get rid of a persecuting God. The "true God" that I refer to in that paper is not like that. I think you have to read the scriptures too, both the New Testament and the Old Testament, to see there is this constant interplay between what I call the "true God" and also the condemning "false God". For instance, near that passage about the prophet Nathan, when David says to him "I have sinned against Yahweh", the Ark of the Covenant is being brought to Jerusalem: "The Ark of the Covenant was on an oxen cart and it tipped and was in danger of falling off and Uzzah put his hand forward to steady it and he was struck down by Yahweh." There you have two quite different types of experience: whereas when David said, "I have sinned against Yahweh", he meant "I have sinned against that sort of principle within", the other is a superstitious type of thing. It is quite different. I think it is necessary in all these religions to differentiate.

There is no harm in talking about the Mafia—or I can think about someone who used to talk about a sort of a robber who was active inside his personality—as long as it is realized that they have had actually some function, and they have some capacity to look after the person. It's as if they have functioned to hold the person together. I mention all this because psychoanalytic institutes are far too narrow and in-looking, and one always needs to be quite careful and suspect when, for instance, our discipline is criticized, that there is usually some truth to it. I am thinking particularly of the recent criticisms by Frederick Crews. I think most of his criticism was ill-informed and certainly not thought out in a very logical way, but what is far more embarrassing were the arguments that were put forward by analysts to defend themselves. Frederick Crews had some truths to say, so why not acknowledge them. Even with behaviourism, which we disagree with because we believe in the internal principles of motivation, but, on the other hand, the external behaviour is an important factor and needs to be attended to, and so behaviourism and cognitive therapy, its progeny, are not all nonsense. I have heard people speaking like this—that the stability of the analytic session and the sense of knowing that the person will always be there and the steadiness of it is itself a help; those are behavioural principles. What I am trying to get at is that I have been helped enormously by being in audiences where I have been criticized, and I think it is something of a disaster that we are so defensive.

To try to see how this god gets created, I'll give a clinical vignette. One of the features of this narcissistic constellation of madness is extreme hypersensitivity. The sort of God that I am talking about that is so powerful in the personality is a very sensitive creature, and you realize that it is actually *not* quite so powerful once you see him through that lens.

A woman tried to persuade me to tell her whether she should modernize her kitchen or not. Of course, it wasn't put in such a crude way as that. "I just want you to help me clarify the matter", she said. It was one of those occasions where I didn't speak. Now, in fact, it was also quite clear that there was a very powerful impulse—and I use the word impulse—in her to modernize her kitchen. What she wanted me—God—to do was to endorse this impulse, this project. I need to emphasize that I was very firmly established as God in her mind. The question is, why didn't she just do it? Why did she have to get my endorsement? Why did she *need* me to endorse it? This is where it comes to Bion. I think there are two modes of human action. Either we act on impulse, or we act freely. The reason why she tried to get my endorsement was that she was going to act on impulse. Whenever people act on impulse, they are guilty. Why are they guilty? Because it damages them, whereas if they act freely, after things have been processed, it is enriching to the personality. She is going to act on impulse—she is guilty—and so Neville Symington told her it was a good idea to modernize her kitchen. It is quite interesting when one looks at it. I might think to myself, "I am God and very important to this patient", but actually I am a puppet on the end of a string. With this woman, not to act on impulse but to think about it and discuss it with her family, which I think she knew would involve a whole lot of other things—would mean that a big pot would be stirred if it was discussed. So, what I am emphasizing is that there are two modes of action: acting on impulse and evading pain and difficulty, versus acting freely but with a considerable psychic pain and difficulty. So it is when the person is acting on impulse that God gets created. It either gets created outside or inside. A very interesting thing happened after that. This woman went home, and she had a reconciliation with her husband, from whom she had been alienated for more than a year—they had been living apart—and she said afterwards quite definitely, "I felt I took authority into myself." So God was banished, and authority was taken into herself. When she said that she took authority into herself, she tapped her breast to indicate that she had taken it within.

When I talk about God in this way, God is always embodied, either in the person, or not just in the analyst or therapist, but also in *others* as well. So, for instance, in an extreme case, if the analyst is a man, say, it might be embodied in all men, including the analyst. It is not ever embodied just in one individual. It might be embodied in all analysts, or all doctors. I mention this because I think a clinical mistake is quite often made where the analyst hears someone talking in a hostile way about, let's say, Dr J, or whoever it is, and he thinks that stands for him. That is not correct. It stands for him and that person as a merged entity. It is quite an important difference, and it also means that the patient is also merged with the analyst, that is why I put the glue there (Intensifiers—see frontispiece). There is a glue-like attachment. The assumption that there is an individual there is not so; and what is most powerfully resisted in all this is a meeting with the analyst as *person*, because if the analyst as *person* is met, then it forces the individual to create himself into a person. However, it also faces the individual with the terror of meeting a savage and crushing God within. The moment that comes inside is a dangerous one and can lead to suicide. It is also one of the reasons why I said that there is such a powerful resistance to seeing deficits of character in the analyst. If the black and the white are seen, it is exceedingly difficult for the person to manage it. Someone has asked me about people who have influenced me. Apart from Bion, whom you have often heard me mention, the philosopher John Macmurray says that "It is through a creative interaction with the other person that the person really comes to birth." I am not sure he realized, though, what a terror this can be for the individual who is plagued by a fiercesome God.

I just want to say one other thing, which I think fits in here better than anywhere else, and that is about perversion. If we look at it according to this whole schema, the question of what is perverse and what is not can, I think, only be solved by scrutinizing the emotional activity, of which sexual activity is a sign. Normality and perversity in sexual mores cannot be determined by the outer activity alone. Sexual intercourse between a man and a woman cannot be called normal on the basis of just the physical act. If it is done, for example, with emotional tenderness, it is different from being done with hostile vengeance. Once we look at it in this way, the very words "normal" and "perverse" seem to come out of the wrong mindset, and really our categories here of sane and mad seem to be more appropriate. So according to my schema and the underlying emotional situation, if there is one where there is an absence of emotional giving, then perversion is around. It may be replaced by something that looks like giving at the surface level. So if one thinks of it in this way, then perversion, the need for the other to gratify, tends to dominate the sexual drama, and the partner is being used, maybe, as a masturbatory tool. Perversion occurs, said Freud, when some form of foreplay became predominant, whereas if it became integrated within an orgasmic whole, it was normal. I want to translate this into emotional terms and say that sexual activities are healthy if they are integrated within an interpersonal drama of mutual giving. Then, of course, you have to solve the problem of whether you think homosexual activity can express mutual giving and therefore be normal. I don't think the defining feature of perversity is to be found in the external acts. Like all these things, you can obviously run the thing too far, and there could be some sort of very exploitative form of paedophilia or something that would be difficult to think of being susceptible to any emotional giving. I know it is always dangerous, and phrases like "emotional giving" are vague and susceptible to self-deception, but I think it is quite important to try to get another angle on it.

There is another important angle about it that is quite closely likened to what I said about Bion's use of the dichotomy between evading and modifying pain. I'll just try and explain it in this way. A man's mother died giving birth to him. He was a lonely man who spent much of his time at blue movies. He longed for me to make emotional contact with him, and, as nearly always is the case when someone expresses such a wish, he manoeuvred in every way possible to prevent it happening. What gave him a particular buzz was to go to a homosexual brothel and offer himself passively to another man, and then, just as he was about to be penetrated, he would close himself up so the man's penis could not penetrate. This gave him a buzz. It was a representation of actually what he was wanting—i.e. the penis penetrating equalling the desire for emotional contact. It was as if he were holding up a picture of what he wanted and how he stopped it happening. The perversity lay in the fact that awareness of the painful emotional situation between him and me was being avoided, but the point I want to make is this: if you just said, "Oh, well, that's totally perverse, absolutely perverse", you'd actually get it wrong, because you'd miss the fact that something good is being attempted but not being achieved because a wrong direction has been taken. One can also see in the perversion the intensity of the pain that was involved for him in making emotional contact with me—the pain of an elemental loss. I thought I was on the road that would bring me to the Tavistock but found myself at Kenwood House instead. My desire was not wrong, but I took the wrong road. It is enormously important that a Godly judgement is avoided, because it is the Godly judgement that brings "the worm". It is exceedingly difficult to avoid, but I think that technically one of the ways one needs to approach this is slowly to interpret the different aspects of the whole drama, so the thing slowly begins to be integrated without a hint of hatred.

The way god gets created in the individual is the way it gets created in our religions and the mystics set themselves to the task of getting a true god rather than this false one installed in consciousness.

> *Floor:* I'd like to ask something about what happened when you were talking about paedophilia. I very much go along with what you were saying about the emotional giving; it makes a lot of sense to me. I was wondering in contrast to the *extreme* that you mentioned, and that no doubt we would all agree with—is it possible to imagine a kind of paedophiliac activity that *does* give to the child what the child *needs*?

I think it is possible. It is very difficult. I think there are various things one has to think of. To start with, when anything of this sort happens, the emotional reaction is usually shocked horror in some way or another. I think one does need to get past that to try to see what is really happening. I certainly think that the type of witch-hunt mentality that exists at the moment with relation to people who have committed paedophiliac acts is primitive in the extreme. We need to try to understand these things, and so I could imagine a situation where some benefit could occur.

> *Floor:* One has to assume that not all children are totally traumatized by the experience, that there are loving aspects to it. But what I think I am trying to focus on is that, I don't know quite how to express it—it has to be, surely, that an adult who can't contain their own feeling or is seeking fulfilment through a child is putting onto the child all their own unresolved conflict.

Yes.

> *Floor:* And I think what bothers me is the violence of breaking down the barrier which ought to exist between adult and child, and obviously tolerance of the individual is what we need. I absolutely agree with you about the witch hunts, but to say that raises an enormous moral problem; I am not sorry I am raising an enormous moral problem, but condoning it is something else, isn't it?

Oh, yes, I'm not condoning it. What I am trying to say is that the way one defines perversity needs to be based on the emotional content of the act, and there are sexual acts that I find difficult to think could ever be expressive of emotional giving. One can think of the most terribly violent sexual acts that end in murder and stuff—it is difficult to think that any of those could be normal. However, what I am saying is that the way one defines normal as opposed to perverse needs to rest upon the inner emotional content. So, for instance, sexual intercourse between two people who are properly married can be perverse.

> *Floor:* I absolutely agree with everything you have said. Maybe

a slight example from my own practice long ago will help fill this out a bit, because when you said that about murderous activities etc., I think the path of compassion has to tell us that we have to keep trying to understand and be compassionate about these things. I did once have a patient who had all sorts of problems, among which, alongside all the other things he engaged in, he liked to be in bed with a couple—a heterosexual couple—but only if they were beating each other up. This obviously related to the events of his childhood, which is the only significant one that I can see. Although it was a very disrupted childhood and he had a very manipulative father, the important thing, as I saw it, was that his mother was a Christian Scientist. I can, thinking back about this as a sort of vignette rather than an accurate description of the man, I *can* see that murderous activity is his path to realization, if you like, in part, which is a very difficult area. But while I am talking I am also thinking of the Baron de Charlier in *Remembrance of Things Past*—you know, he is quite a good example of there being something else at the heart of perverse activity.

Yes, I tend to think that. I am not sure if this is quite right, but this is my interpretation of Freud. It seems to me in some of Freud's later papers the heart of perversion is masochism and sadism really, and even there, let's say in the case of the sexually sadistic act or masochistic act, the much more important thing is the emotional sadism that it represents. My understanding is that it always means that there is an emotional correlate, to that which may not be an exact translation. There is always an emotional correlate, and that's the really serious matter. I do think there is a tendency to look at the sexual and not look at the emotional. I don't know if it is true, but I remember reading that Hitler used to get a great sexual buzz from lying on the ground and getting a woman to urinate on him; the correlate of that is him urinating on the Jews, so quite how it translates is the serious thing. The sexual is minor; the emotional is major. I can think of quite a number of other cases, but there is a tendency always to be attracted into the sexual and ignore the emotional.

Floor: I wanted to ask your help, and indeed everybody else's help, with thinking about my personal antipathy for organized religion, of which my main experience has been the Anglican faith, and with particular reference to the worm. It seems to me, as I understood it, that I am required to be a worm. I am required to be a miserable sinner, in need of forgiveness before we start, and so if I *am* required to be a miserable sinner that rather gets in the way of my personal acknowledgement of needing help with things that I have come to regard as sinful.

My best answer to that is that within Christian theology there are two very different theories of redemption. The first one goes like this—that when Adam sinned, it was an offence, an infinite offence against God, and so God sent his Son because an infinite offence could only be repaid by someone of the same stature and nature as God Himself, who is Himself infinite. Therefore the whole drama of Calvary, etc. was to repay back to God on Man's behalf an infinite offence. That is one theory of redemption. I might say that it is a theory of redemption that is very pervasive. The other theory of redemption was that God looked down and saw that man had damaged himself and sent His son to try to repair Man's state. Quite different. The sort of thing you are talking about comes from the first theory, and that first one is absolutely in line with what I was saying, because what sort of a God is it that is going to take offence like this, like a sensitive soul offended at a cocktail party? It's just absolute nonsense. So I think that whole thing that you are talking about is part of that system—you are a worm. It is to be repudiated.

Floor: But of course there is also the requirement to be a particular kind of child—a child without curiosity.

Yes. I will say this, though. I have been quite struck in recent years that in any scientific discipline there are quite strict canons and boundaries, and you can think for yourself as long as you don't go beyond a certain point. It is not only within religion that this occurs. I was brought up within the Roman Catholic Church, which has all sorts of strictures: "You can't believe this", and "You can't think that", etc. Slightly more recently I have come to think that at least the Catholic Church was open about it, whereas various scientific disciplines have very powerful taboos: "You must not think this way" and "You must not think that way", but it is much more covert. There is a group of scientists (Bob Jahn in America is one of them) who have the view that a human observing presence can affect inanimate objects. He has been excommunicated by the scientific community. I have no problem if they say, "Listen, put this to the test, and if it is wrong, OK, it's wrong"—but it is not that. He's banished without trial. I have come across the same thing among philosophers, among psychologists, among anthropologists. So I think it is much more widespread than we realize—only that in religions it is more obvious. I think there is what I call a "bad religious principle" active in almost all fields of knowledge.

> *Floor:* I have thought about it a lot, and I actually think that this first bit that you described in the first theory is actually a perversion, in almost a literal sense of the word—a twisting away from the real meaning—and I have come back to the Anglican faith, but only on the basis of the second view of redemption. But I am quite passionate in belief and understanding with the diverse quality in the first theory.

Well, I think the first theory comes straight out of that bit I gave you about the woman who was wanting to act on impulse and had me as a God to endorse it. I think it is part of that system, and I agree, I think it is, and what is needed is for that system to be transformed.

> *Floor:* I want to go back to the question of paedophilia. I think the speaker and yourself were talking mainly from the point of view of the adult and how it is important not to go through a witch hunt of the paedophile, etc., because I think it is quite disturbing, what you said. I hope I am not reacting in a sort of moralistic way, but from the child's point of view I would say that any act which implies a sexual action between an adult and a child cannot have a positive side, even if it is a loving act, even if it is a sexual, loving, tender, gentle, act but between an adult and a child, as I think most people here would agree. I can't save anything which is acceptable, in a sense, because there is massive infringement of boundaries, which is

an abusive act in itself. Hence it becomes a perverse act, even if there is loving, and paedophiles are renowned for being very loving, very tender, and I have seen adults who had years of sexual abuse from loving paedophiles and how damaged they are, with their children, also. So I don't want you to go out of this audience thinking that you believe that something can be saved in a paedophile act, in a sexual act between a child and an adult.

I want to come back to the other point that I made: what is the traumatic thing that is so disturbing for a child? I would like to emphasize that if that is happening, what is it that is not happening?

Floor: I have got so many things going through my head about what you are saying. I am *not* an analyst, and I don't come from an analytic tradition, but I am very struck by some of the things that you say. I am trying to make connections and discriminations between those and the things I am more familiar with, and I think I need to check a couple of things out with you. I have a sense of the path that you are treading as something to do with the tension between, on the one hand, a sort of fragmented individualism, and, on the other hand, a kind of fundamentalist totalitarianism, which I think is something to do with the bad God, and I am struck by your use of the word "conscience". I am wondering if there are connections between your idea of conscience and what I would understand as a search for an authenticity which is not linked with individualistic voluntarism, but which is a sense of authenticity that has to do with the connection of the absolute, the infinite—the being in which we all participate, if you like. So there is something about the connection between or difference between, your sense of conscience and a notion of authenticity.

The other one that struck me was that you have talked about contact and becoming a person through contact with the other, and also contact with or a sense of God through contact with the other, and the thing that strikes me there is that there may be some connection with Buber's notion of the

I–Thou relationship, and I just really wanted to check a couple of those things out because I don't know if I am in a different universe or if there are connections.

It is a strange paradox that when you look at someone and you say "Well, they're authentic", it's an authenticity that has arisen through having been chosen, and the choosing of it is what endows it with its authenticity. That, to my mind, is related directly to conscience, which comes as an inner invitation. I find it a bit more difficult to try to get across the thing about the person-to-person and the I–Thou. I think the personality is made up of all these elements, and when this sort of system is in operation with God condemning and so on, parts of the personality are in other people, other people are in the personality, and there is a confused mix-up. You don't have a person. You have a unit in an amorphous mass. The taking possession of all the different parts is not just taking possession of them, but, rather, a creative act has to occur that brings them into a unity. It is like paints on a palette, and they are brought together in a pattern, in a design, through the painter's creative act. But that creative act can only occur in relation to what I refer to as the infinite but as encountered in the other and so you can think of it in this way: there is an interrelation of creation and of persons.

When the other is in any way invested with godhead, then that inhibits and cripples, but there is this other process going on whereby a creative process is occurring. It does occur between two persons—actually, the right way to put it is "two becoming persons" is how it takes place. I don't know if that answers the question. I only read Buber's *I and Thou* once, not twice, and so I can't comment really. I'm sure it is an important book, but it didn't have a strong echo in me for some reason.

Floor: ... in a therapeutic relationship ...

Yes, I certainly think that is so. I am quite certain that is so. I have seen the odd person very infrequently and I remember seeing someone for quite a period once in three months, and a definite process was occurring and there were quite significant moments of realization and development, and I am quite certain of this: those significant moments of realization are a crystallization of something, and they are of tremendous importance. I can think of occasions where suddenly there has been an understanding, and you are changed by it, and you are never the same person again. I remember when doing philosophy years ago, this man saying: "I am only interested in what you understand, and when the exams come, I am not interested in you using your memory." It is something to do with that, really. I think acts of understanding are enormously important, but they are at a premium in today's society. We are so *bombarded* with facts and information, and it goes against understanding, but those moments of understanding are clearly crucial. That picture of the Baptism of Christ is an outer symbol of a moment of inner realization.

Floor: I have two remarks to make: one is the relationship with the analyst. I am just a patient, yes? Just a patient.

Just? Just?

Floor: No, no, it's coming, it's coming! And the other is this relationship with God. You said something which really struck me: you said, "What sort of God would it be if it would take offence?" It was a bit joking but in a way I think this is very important because if you talk about a God which is not that one in that game there, but the one we try to approach in this search for understanding of the absolute and infinite, that God either doesn't have qualities of not being offended, or, if we really want to have a relationship, in my mind, I take your sentence in which you said—and this was very important to me—that it is a creative interaction with another person—that the person comes to birth, and in a way it is the same business with God. Thomas Mann has a very good description about how the idea of God comes from people, so it is people who create God. Yes? So in my mind God must have human attributes such as anger and the ability to be offended, or it is very difficult to have a relationship with him. That's one thing.

The other thing is the relationship with the analyst. I thought it was very helpful for me to hear that really it is when there is a creative interaction with another person that a person comes to birth, and it was a very important thing that you said. The situation is that the set-up—and probably all you analysts and therapists have thought about it a lot of times—but the set-up is such that it is very difficult for a patient to have knowledge about the analyst, because the analyst has to be guessed and is not known, we do not know the analyst. I can't see the analyst in certain situations, so the set-up is a very disturbing one in which to achieve a *good* goal such as you mentioned.

This sort of God, like the one in the example where the lady had this impulse to modernize her kitchen and wanted me as God to endorse it: The sense of being offended—and it is paradoxical—is precisely being very easily offended and hurt and that one's sensibilities have been wounded that goes together with a God of this nature, so it is like a false one. The infinite, the absolute—which can be grasped through an act of understanding that's not the result of a sudden sort of illumination on the road to Damascus or like Mohammed suddenly receiving a catastrophic trance—if you want to talk about God being offended, then one is in the realm of this false one, this one with power that can't bear pain and so on.

The other thing that you said about the analytic setting: there are a couple of things, I think, to be said here. About the business of the actual setting, I'll tell you a story which perhaps might illustrate it. I had a patient, a woman, who used to lie on the couch, but she quite often used to say, "I somehow feel it would be much better if I got up or sat down or whatever", and following my type of policy, I didn't say, "Well, why not?" because there was obviously some difficulty and barrier for her in it, but I also didn't say anything to discourage her from doing so. Then it emerged that she had lain down in the first place on the couch because someone had said to her, "It's not a decent analysis unless you lie down on the couch", because she had started by sitting up. I didn't know at this stage that she had been told that, so she thought, "I must have a decent analysis and lie down on the couch." Once she had repudiated this group mentality within, she then felt free, and this was a healthy moment.

* * *

The purpose of the little visual aid called "Intensifiers" (frontispiece) is one of the problems I keep coming back to. It is that it is very difficult to conceptualize something in such a way that one realizes that in this system all is in everything, so that when I talk about those liquifiers or intensifiers—greed, envy, and jealousy—of course the God that one is talking about is imbued with all three of these. It comes out in that paper, "The True and the False God" (Appendix A). It is a greed-envious-jealous God that interferes with, prevents creativity, and so on, and so it is terribly important to differentiate that from what I call the true God—the infinite, the absolute, ultimate truth—that all realities *is*. One of the underlying themes of this conference is that there is a false god that strangles personal growth and creativity and a true god that promotes them. Incidentally, this adherence to one or the other has little relevance to whether someone is consciously theist or atheist. I have had atheist patients adhering to the true god or the false god. I have had believers who adhere to one or the other. Everyone is governed by these principles, whatever their overt belief might be.

The other thing that you said, about the analytic setting—there are a couple of things, I think, to be said here. Analysts are nervous before their patients arrive. I don't know if you ever realized that, but they often are. Bion said, "If the analyst is not nervous then there is something wrong", and the reason he said that was "Because before the patient walks into the consulting-room you don't know what's going to happen, or what is going to suddenly confront you." And he said, "That in itself is unnerving." Analysts do protect themselves against that to some extent by being stiff, rigid, having a sort of posture. I remember when I was working at the Tavistock in the adult department, and I used to walk along the corridor, and the doors were open, and therapists or analysts were standing in their rooms, and you could always tell if they were waiting for a patient or not. If they were waiting for a patient, they were a little more rigid and tense, but I think that is one thing. So the ideal thing, obviously, is for the analyst or therapist to be as relaxed as possible and therefore as receptive to what's going to happen as possible, that's the ideal. But I think you have to remember that analysts are human beings, and they may be anxious and therefore a bit rigid and so on.

The other business about not knowing the analyst—that's not true. You know a great deal about the analyst—a great deal. The way they dress, all sorts of things, the sorts of cars they drive. The other thing that I do think is that you don't *know* people from knowing their biographical history. I think there are many more clues that are available than perhaps people realize.

Now, someone else asked me a question about religion. I think the question was about organized religion being very much made up of a sense of an inner jelly and a crust. I don't think that is completely true. The extent to which someone is governed by that inner constellation, to that extent they may make a crust out of the external rules and still be an inner jelly inside. I mean I think the sign of it is in my book, *Emotion and Spirit*. I keep coming back to this thing of trying to get to the sort of inner pearl of great price that *is* within the great religions, and I have no doubt that all the great religions have a great treasure—not only a great treasure, but also a great psychological wisdom inside them, but there are a whole lot of peripheral things that are capable of superstitious type of attachment, and so it is like all great religious leaders and innovators: they have a series of disciples, and then slowly a process of rigidification sets in.

There are two other questions. One was this business of God and the worm; someone was saying that religious people want this. There is often a very strong attachment to this system, and it has often held the person together, and they have survived through it, and they are afraid to let go of it. To let go takes an act of faith—a trusting act, which may end in disaster. What moves someone to make an act of trust is impossible to answer.

And the last question someone asked is "What is God?" I don't think I can answer just like that, because the whole conference is *about* that. I just think that one has to try to absorb what that really is about.

> *Floor:* Could we come back to that either now or later, because I felt very uneasy with your response to the first thing which was raised initially about the issue of the attributes of God and can God be offended, or what kind of God is it who has greed, envy, and jealousy as part of Him. I didn't feel that you

INTENSIFIERS

(illustration: a circle labeled GOD overlaid with the words CREED, ENVY, JEALOUSY)

made good enough sense of that, because then just to say "Well, there is a good kind of God—the absolute the infinite" and *then* what? I mean, that's not an answer to what you were coming to—what is God? But it seems to me that the issue is that if there is a dialogue that you think about for creativity with God or between people, then it has to do with owning or including. It is necessary to go more fully into what you mean by the absolute, the infinite, and why we are using both those words, absolute and infinite, all the time. It just needs to kind of—I would like there to be a kind of fuller discussion about that, because that is a very big issue. That's *the* central issue of what enables the creative act. I would like there to be a bit more of that, I mean I think what Eva said at the beginning—can a God who is offended and yet deal *differently* with his own feeling of being offended, or does God have . . .

This brings me, then, to the first question that was asked: not understanding about God being offended. You see, this sort of God, like the one I explained, where the lady had this impulse to modernize her kitchen and wanted me as God to endorse it. The sense of being offended—and it is paradoxical—it is precisely being very sort of easily offended and hurt and that one's sensibilities have been wounded goes together with a God of this nature, so it is like a false one. The infinite, the absolute, which can be grasped through an act of understanding, that's not the result of a sudden sort of illumination on the road to Damascus.

I think even talking like that means you are in the wrong register. I keep going back to the seers of the Upanishads, because I think there was a new birth of consciousness at that time that went across cultures. There were the seers of the Upanishads, the early Hebrew prophets, there was Socrates in Greece; it has been referred to as the Axial Era. There was a new dawning of consciousness, and I think what all these people had was a deep understanding of what reality is, and *how* it is, and how they are constituted as a part of it. That is why, when Bion refers to it, he refers to the infinite, or the absolute, or truth. These are approximate words to try to describe what these people were on about and their vision. That is quite different from the notion of an all-powerful figure who directs and who suddenly knocked St Paul off his horse. In the Bible you get an interplay the whole time between the one and the other. I am not a biblical scholar, but I am sure you could do a progressive analysis of the Bible to show how the idea purified as it went along, and I think that has been done. But there is always this tendency to go back to what is basically a false God, a powerful figure that dictates and overrides the creative inner power of conscience.

> *Floor:* I see another picture, and I may not have expressed myself fully and clearly about what I was thinking about the other God. I was not thinking about that scheme, and I understand what you mean by that. The picture I have—and it may be helpful—is somewhat like it is sort of Jacob's Ladder, yes? There is something which we *sort of* understand, which is the infinite and the absolute, and there is another thing we seem to understand which is the particular and the varied and differentiated, and our mystery is that we see God in both sides. And I think what I was talking about—that we sometimes see God as an infinite God or whatever—sometimes we see the absolute and the infinite, and sometimes we see the

differentiated and the particular, and the differentiated and the particular can be the God which we imagine. I am sorry to say it is not my idea, but it is God like. For example, in the Jewish religion God sometimes is angry, yes? There are bits of this as well. So somehow our feeling is just as mysterious, so whether we go up or we go down or we are up or we look down . . .

Yes, but I think we need to be careful, because in the Bible there is this strange interplay between an anthropomorphic idea of God and a much purer one. The prophets went on and on and on about not making statues, not erecting something. In other words, that you could not imagine this, and so there they were actually talking about the infinite. Words like "the infinite" mean "not finite", it is a negative type of described thing, it is saying "*not* this". Moses Maimonides was, I think, the first person to formulate what was called the *via negativa*—that all you could talk about were the things that were *not*—so you do have this strange interplay. It is very clear in the prophets, when they were castigating the people for going off after false gods. I don't think it was so much false gods, but making statues of them, and Moses came down the mountain and was furious because they had built a golden calf, always wanting an image. So the sense was that this is *not* something that can be imagined. Then, when you get these other things about God being angry, that's not correct, you see. That's a much more primitive image. What might be right is that the people had acted against their inner principles and *therefore* suffered from it, but it wasn't that there was a God there, saying, "You are naughty children, you know, and we are now going to send the Babylonians to take you into captivity." It wasn't that. It is important to get that difference. It's the same in the Gospels—you get that same interplay going on the whole time, and the mystics were aware of this. You might say, "Well, surely, then the vision of the seers of the Upanishads—That Thou Art—was by far the best, and let's leave aside the whole Judaeo-Christian thing", but I don't think that's right because something was revealed within the Judaeo-Christian dispensation that is relating to the personal, which didn't really ever come out in the Eastern tradition. We are coming up to the second millennium, and it is a time to try to draw out the good from all these great religions and, I think, be prepared, without being disrespectful, of being able to say that there are superstitious or anthropomorphic elements here and there, and there is no need to be offensive, but they are not really essential—the important thing is to recognize what the reality is that is being spoken about. To speak of a God being offended is an image, like the golden calf, from which we need to purify ourselves.

> *Floor:* Can I just say that if the infinite is personal, then, without being anthropomorphic, surely the infinite must then have some kind of response—not necessarily a human one, but feelings like love or indignation at seeing terrible injustice or some feelings of concern for what happens, rather than just a completely faceless therapist, as it were, without any responses.

Oh, come on now, look at that thing I quoted from Didier Houzel with the therapist who sat in the bathroom—that wasn't a faceless therapist, you see, that was a concerned therapist. I think I'll just leave you with that, really.

MEDITATION SIX

Trauma and attachment

There we are: "glue" (see Intensifiers—frontispiece). We are all quite used to talking about separation and the effect of separation and the effect of loss. However, in this constellation one of the elements that is always, always present is what I call a "glue-like attachment". It is the only way I can describe it. I think it is similar to what Mrs Bick used to call "adhesive identification". Now, I want to explain something. I put paranoia at the opposite end of it. You see, when there is that glue-like attachment—and I'll try to describe a bit more what I mean by the glue-like attachment in a moment—I think it is very important to go back to this central point that what human beings seek is freedom. If I am attached in a glue-like way to somebody, to my mother or father or whatever, I'm entrapped, and there is a hatred of being in that entrapped state, but it is not the way I experience it. The way I experience it is that I hate the figure. So let's say I am attached to my mother in a glue-like way, I hate *her*, you see, and someone might say "Well, *why* do you hate her?"—"Oh, well, she is so possessive and she is so arrogant and she's exploitative and she doesn't take any interest in me" or whatever, and all those things *may* be true—probably are. I haven't yet come across a mother without deficits. However, what is actually hated is the glue-like attachment to either an individual or an individual merged in the group. So that is how you get the paranoia, and the paranoia is always associated with that glue-like attachment. I defy you to produce an example of someone who is paranoid who doesn't have a glue-like attachment to an institution, a school of thinking, a group, or something. It is part and parcel of the same type of system. This is the thing that is difficult to grasp, but it is also part of the system of "God and the Worm" as well. I am just, as it were, bringing the lens round to look at this side of it.

The other important thing is that when we look for images of this, people very often talk about the infant at the breast, and I think that the image is misleading. It's not sufficient for what I am talking about. It is an attachment that is far more bonded, far more imprisoned. It may be because I am living in Australia, but the best possible image that I can think of is the kangaroo when it gives birth to its tiny infant, and it comes out, an inch long, a tiny little thing, which crawls up and places itself in the pouch. That to my mind is a far better image of what I am talking about, because its very survival rests on that. I have a photograph—it's not very good unfortunately. Can you see that? Can you see the little head poking out? That's quite a big one, and it might even be able to jump out of the pouch and exist for a bit, but on the other hand you wouldn't see a photograph of one when it was tiny. I think this is a very important thing clinically, because the trauma of separation is only a trauma if the *attachment* is of this nature—a glue-like sort—and when there is this sort of attachment, interpretations are heard as directives. In my paper, "The Corruption of Interpretation through Narcissism" there is a study of a woman who showed some of the manifestations of the attachment. She would ring at the weekends and listen to my voice on the answer phone. During breaks she would hold onto one of my books. In such an attachment one always finds intense hatred. There is terrific shame about it too. This situation once happened. She left the consulting-room, and I was free for a while subsequent to her departure. I went out of the consulting-room, and I turned first right, first right again, first right again, and right again into our bank which just backs onto the consulting-room, so it is exactly behind our building.

When I got there, she was also in the bank, and she didn't notice me until one of the bank-tellers who knew me quite well said, "Oh, hello Mr Symington", so she then saw me. Certain things happened the next time she came, and I made an interpretation to her along these lines: I said that I push her rudely out of the consulting-room, and she comes round into the back/bank door, and I said, "It is like a little child looking into the parents' bedroom"—some interpretation of that nature. She was absolutely mortified by that, and one can question whether it was the right thing to have said or not, but it did produce a tremendous emotional outpouring. It was that picture of herself like a little 'roo attached that she hated. She hated being attached in that way, and why? Because it restricted her freedom. One quite valuable thing did come out of it: it was possible for her to see the nature of this attachment and her hatred of it, and then she came to realize that a loathing that she had for her father was partly because of this attachment, and that the various characteristics of her father had been blown up into a huge size. The defects in the object become greatly magnified in this situation.

There is another little bit to this which I also think is quite important to realize. When you get that type of glue-like attachment, there is always a most savage voice that sneers and says, "Look at you, you miserable little creature, that's *all* you are, just a little snivelling parasite", and she clearly thought I was saying, "You should not be in that bank. It's *my* bank, you know." What I am trying to get at is that when there is this glue-like attachment, there is this *fearful* voice that is condemning of it. Why is there always this condemning voice? I think it is because the patient has attached herself to the place of the analyst's deficit, and this is the reason why it is crucial that the analyst's own deficits become elucidated. As soon as the analyst's deficit becomes elucidated, the pathological attachment can no longer be maintained. It's like a tree fungus that attaches itself to that part of the tree where the sap is coming out. Then there is guilt and shame about attaching at the point of vulnerability. I hide my own deficit by burying in the deficit of another. Let's say it is arrogance or omnipotence or greed. When the analyst's deficit can be discovered, that is the place where the attachment can take place, and the thing is then hidden—it is like hiding your own wound in the wound of another. I think that is the reason why the person gets such a shocking sense of castigation.

All those are not discreet, they are interconnected, and so it is a whole type of a system (see frontispiece). The question is this: how has all that come about? This is where I depart from Melanie Klein on this. Melanie Klein tended to take the view that envy, particularly, was rooted in the constitution in some way, as if it were an inherited thing. I came to notice that people who had undergone the very worst traumas were the people in whom this whole system was most firmly ensconced. Precisely the sort of person who is most obviously envious, greedy, ambitious, impossible, nasty, provocative, is someone who has been traumatized. I came to think of it even a bit differently from that in a paper called "Narcissism as Trauma Preserved". In Bion's *Theory of Transformation* he starts off by saying that a painter is looking at a lake surrounded by meadows and trees and so on—let's say the scene in front of him covers ten acres—and then the painter gets a canvas one foot square, and with some paints—blue and green and white—he makes a representation of what is in front of him. Bion makes the point that there has been a transformation from one to the other, although if you look at it, the two are totally different. One is a few bits of paint on a tiny little bit of canvas, while the other is grass, trees, etc. covering an area of ten acres. Similarly, when you see this whole set-up, it is not only the result of the trauma—I think it *is* the trauma in living form. The people around you get projected into, and so they experience the trauma. When you get some of these appalling disasters—in Australia some years ago there was a chap at Port Arthur who went berserk and shot 22 people, and shock waves went right through the Australian community—that's a gross example, but there's the trauma. In lesser cases one can take it that this whole system is the trauma. I think it is quite an important perspective, because it does, without doubt, alter one's view of it and understanding of it. When I wrote the book on narcissism, I did have a chapter on trauma, but I didn't understand it in this way at that time. I am absolutely certain that understanding it more now in the way that I do is therapeutically far more beneficial. And it doesn't mean in any way that one colludes with all the manipulative manoeuvres and so on, but it does give one some sort of an understanding that this is the way the trauma now lives in the soul of the person, if you like.

I think if one tries to get what a trauma is exactly, the best description I have seen is in *The Diary of Anne Frank*. I always think the saddest moment in that book is a little statement added by the editor at the end, that Anne Frank's sister fell from the top bunk in the concentration camp, and that the fall killed her. The editor says, "That did to Anne Frank what all else was unable to do—it broke her spirit, and she died." I think that fundamentally a trauma is when a person's spirit is broken. When I talk about the jelly-like state, *that* is the trauma. Something has occurred that has broken their spirit. It may have all sorts of different manifestations—somatic, and all the other types of manifestations that one knows about—but when someone comes to the consulting-room, there are obviously some embers left that are in hope that something can arise from within and start to put these pieces together again. There is also a tremendous force against it the whole time because whenever things have shattered out of some pain, as they are put together again, the pain is re-experienced. Again I want to go back to what I said at the beginning: the actual acts that bring parts together, if the analyst acts as god or is god or lets that happen, then the bits, or the jelly, stays as it is really, and a hard crust is kept on the outside, so it is a question of a slow process whereby some—what one might call the spirit of life—comes and begins to bring the different fragmented parts together again. As each emotional act occurs—call it trust, faith, act of generosity, whatever—then this system begins, instead of acting against the personality, to transform it instead.

Gordon Lawrence reminded me that I hadn't said anything about something I used to refer to when I gave lectures here at the Tavistock years ago as "the tragic position". I used to take Melanie Klein's "paranoid position" and "depressive position" and then added another, which is what I call "the tragic position". This is where what one might call life's circumstances come into play. I might try and give an example of this. I was treating a man who came from the Northern Territory in Australia, and it happened that he had to be in Sydney for quite a long time, and so he came for analysis, but he had a triple infantile trauma. One was that he was a twin—a mother has more difficulty in attending to two—and another was that he was born premature, and the third was that he was in an incubator for the first six weeks of his life. He was very abusive, and if ever I made an interpretation, he used to say, "You're just a pommie bastard" and every type of abuse. But I also noticed that he abused himself just as much: he used to refer to himself as a load of shit and useless and so on, so I realized these two things were parallel. As I began to look at this situation at the time of his birth, which was more than fifty years ago—and I think you can imagine what infant care in a hospital in London might have been like fifty years ago, but if you imagine the Northern Territory in Australia, I mean, Bowlby wouldn't have been heard of, or any type of care of that sort. He was *fearfully* paranoid and abusive to me and to his parents and so on, but slowly, as this situation began to be tackled, some quite touching things began to emerge. His mother, when he was in the incubator, used to express the milk from her breasts. They were a family on slender resources, and the father would take this milk in bottles, and take two buses to the hospital, and through the nurses he would feed it to the two babies in the incubators. So even that in a way was quite remarkable, I thought, that a mother had the prescience to trouble to do this. What I am trying to get at is that it is far, far easier to blame me, the parents, everyone else for his situation, but this is where the tragic position comes in. To realize that his parents had actually done their best in the circumstances, and probably the hospital too, given their knowledge at the time and so on: they were trying to save the lives of these two young premature twins. If he had been born fifty or sixty years later and been in different circumstances, perhaps the treatment of him would have been far better. But whom can you blame in that situation? In fact, from my understanding of it, given the circumstances of the time, the parents—and I doubt if they had very much psychological understanding—acted with remarkable concern and care. He was also left slightly handicapped as a result of all this, but I think what comes in is what Gordon Lawrence was reminding me of: that is what I call the tragedy of human existence. It was far more difficult for this chap to come to realize that than to blame someone, and not only someone, but me, his parents, or himself, than to realize that the circumstances were, for him, tragic. No one could be blamed for it. It is as the philosopher Bergson said: when a primitive man was walking along the mountainside and a boulder came rolling down the hill and by chance hit him and knocked him down and killed him, the general sense was that an enemy had done this. It is far, far more difficult to realize that it was just an event over which there is no control—that is why I bring in the business about the *bad* image of God. It is the idea that you can control something, and perhaps if you killed a sheep and offered it up as a sacrifice, you could control some of these things.

I haven't spoken very long about trauma, but it is absolutely integral to this whole system, and I wouldn't like you to think that the length of time spent on it is a measure of its importance.

> *Floor:* Just to clarify a point in that last example you gave. Did you say that there was a blaming of God, and therefore this separation from the absolute?

Let's get things clear here between what I refer to as the infinite, the absolute, or what one might call a true God as opposed to a false God. He blamed me, he blamed his parents, but it wasn't blaming human beings with their limitations doing what they could. It was blaming godlike figures who could magically have done something about this. It is when that begins to dissolve that then the natural tragedy of the situation makes itself felt.

> *Floor:* In that case, would you expect someone to be unable to deal with the tragic aspects of it and essentially be forever separated because of such a tragedy that they are not willing to accept this dimension of human existence and say "No, that means that there is an awful God and life is awful . . ."

Oh, it's certainly much easier to deal with it that way, but I think it is related to what I gave in that other example of the sort of quick-fix way of trying to solve it rather than actually having to try to come to terms with this sort of tragedy. In a strange way this is more obvious, say, when an earthquake occurs, when it is obvious that no one can be blamed, but even there you do see people start blaming: "Oh, the houses should have been built better, and the local government should have put better reinforcements in there" etc.—that nearly always happens. It is very difficult for human beings to deal with that.

> *Floor:* You have spoken quite a bit, not so much in this meditation but earlier, about the draining of values from our contemporary society using various allusions. I don't know if I am anticipating what you are going to say or asking you to speak to that topic, but I would love to hear how you make the link between the individual who suffers the narcissistic trauma, the trauma that leads to the narcissistic constellation, which I absolutely agree with—I have done quite a lot of work with what's called post-traumatic stress people, and I absolutely agree with you that it expresses itself in this way—but what is the link between those individuals who, I believe, are widespread among us and often concealed and the society that you feel and I must say I feel we must all take responsibility for because it is in some way infected by this kind of constellation.

I don't think there is any doubt about it: we are not only infected by it, but we endorse it and society endorses it.

Floor: But how has that come about? That is a *huge* question, I know, and I wouldn't expect you to answer it, but how has it occurred, and can we do anything about it?

I often say, you know, that when you get on a public platform, you get asked to answer all the problems of the human race!

Floor: Yes, I'm sorry. I know, it's a huge question, but I think the *link* would be interesting, what the link is between the individual we meet in the consulting-room and the wider society which seems to act against any kind of effort we may make . . .

I'll try to put it in a more positive way. First, to be a prophet of doom for a moment: we clearly live in a culture that endorses all sorts of narcissistic elements, so that is why I made this point at the beginning to Isca. Even conferences are run *against* people having acts of understanding, getting lecturers to give their talks and hand them in six months before, all that sort of thing. What is much wider than that is the degree to which the popular culture is *bombarded* with information, and I guarantee that if two weeks later you ask people what there was in the news, most of it's all gone. A tremendous number of novels and films and so on are shallow, post-modern culture, and a lot of the art is an affront to beauty. I don't mean all of it, but a lot of it nevertheless is, and it's endorsed. And if you agree with me that you only internalize through a creative act, then this passive submission to the information bombardment is an effective vaccination against internalization. That's why I keep stressing that an interpretation doesn't do it, it is the inner creative act that is the agent of internalization, and I think you know that yourself if you think about it enough. So, let's say that we are in this powerless state in modern society, and that the values that are present in the great traditional religions, stretching right back to the Axial era, represent what human beings most need. But there is a positive way of looking at this. Say someone comes to me and says, "Well, look, all that you are saying is that there's great selfishness in the world, but this has always been so. . . ." This is true, and it opens the door to a more optimistic way of looking at it: "Yes, it has always been so, but it has now reached crisis proportions", so it's presenting itself now as a specific which we urgently need to solve. Do you understand what I mean? It's that it has always been there, but when something reaches *appalling* proportions, then the thinkers and men of action wake up and say, "Look, we *must* do something about this." A doom-laden pessimism, where people despair saying that these huge bureaucratic set-ups can't be challenged, smothers the spirit. There was an event in Australia where a big oil company was going to set up a refinery on the Barrier Reef, and just one lone woman went on and on and on and on and on protesting, and finally she won the day. One of my favourite stories is Terence Rattigan's *The Winslow Boy*. The father was determined to bring this bureaucratic system to its knees and acknowledge that his son was innocent of the theft he had been accused of—his still small voice did win through, so I think the present crisis in our culture should be seen as a challenge rather than: "All right, well, let's all lie down and die."

> *Floor:* But do you have a theory as to why it has arisen to such a crisis point? Do you see any antecedents that we can learn anything from?

I can hear someone saying " I do", so let someone else speak!

> *Floor:* I shall be very rash. Before coming to the conference, I went to Swiss Cottage Library in yet another search for the works of Truby King, because I do believe, I mean I am quite paranoid about Truby King, having had a Truby-King trained—or, rather, untrained—nanny. I do believe that the breaking of the baby's spirit, which is what I believe was advocated there, has had that, and the kind of breaking of the human spirit that was shown in the book and film *Regeneration*, for example. I mean, if you are going to have a culture with huge armies and huge conveyor-belt industrial enterprises, you've got to have human beings, so it seems to me, reduced to broken spirits, so that's . . .

Yes, I am sure that's one factor. I think there are multiple factors, but I am sure that's one of them. Another factor is the thing I said in my book, *Emotion and Spirit*: it's this fear of the emotions and emotional activity. The traditional religions have not made good contact with that, and psychoanalysis and the psychotherapies have made an attempt to do so, but they do lack what I call the wisdom that is inherent in the great religions.

> *Floor:* I have also got an idea of one of the contributing factors. It seems to me that we don't accept that pain is necessary, that we have painkillers etc. It was brought home to me in one way by a patient who said to me: "If there's a death, the person has been robbed", and it was only through losing her mother—her mother was 50 when she died—that she then felt she needed to come and get some help, because she totally does not accept reality that involves pain and death, any disease—"somebody's robbing me"—and I think there is an attitude like that . . .

Oh yes, there is.

> *Floor:* . . . nowadays, so we are back to Bion's "evasion of pain" rather than dealing with it.

And there is no doubt that in Freud's theory, as opposed to his actual practice as a human being, and many therapies also are based on hedonistic principles, and the idea that pain, which includes experience of guilt and shame plus loss and mourning, can be anaesthetized is an illusion. There is no anaesthetic, but we devise all kinds of systems to beguile ourselves into believing that there is.

> *Floor:* I'd like to link this point to something that fascinated me in your talk about the anxious attachment being like a fungus and covering up some deficit in the analyst. I agree with everything you've said about the trauma in narcissistic patients, but I do think that there seems to be a correlation also with the trauma having occurred where there is also a narcissistic mother who actually can't bear to be blamed, rightly or wrongly, and sometimes she blames herself because maybe she had her back turned when a particular trauma happened. I could cite several examples of that, and I think the patient actually fears that they can't work through their anger with the analyst because the analyst equally can't bear to be blamed, or can't bear for the patient to know about the ana-

> lyst's actual deficit, just as the mother couldn't bear for the baby to know about the mother's actual deficit. It may or may not have contributed to the trauma in reality, but it is in the fantasy both of the mother and of the baby that the mother's deficit *did* contribute, and that that needs to be worked through.

Well, I think that's perfectly true, because if you think of this schema, then to the extent to which that constellation is operative, the mother can't give emotionally. It is slightly complicated, and it is one of the reasons I think why, in my experience, with this constellation active certainly in the therapeutic situation, the person will look for and sniff out the deficit in the analyst or therapist. That's why I have always said to people when supervising that as soon as you get a strong projective thing beginning to happen, it is necessary to change focus and look into yourself and see actually what's there; that's where the work then has to be done, because it's only when that begins to be processed that some change can occur. No, I think you are right about that, I am sure.

My point is this: one does have to be careful to recognize that the child projects into the mother's narcissism—the mother's narcissism is there, and so is the infant's—and that this projection magnifies it. So you do have to watch for the fact that therefore what gets obliterated from consciousness are the good and healthy elements in the mother and the father. It's important to realize that one's own task is to effect some transformation of this, and my experience is that when that begins to happen, the person might say, "Oh, I do remember, actually my mother always used to give me a special surprise at weekends" or "She used to come and visit me when I was at boarding school", and so on. These good occasions had been blotted out until then—the bad has been magnified and obliterated the good. I was quite moved by this situation once. I was seeing a man who had a tremendous rage towards his father. His hatred was very concrete: that his father had done this and his father had done that and his father had prevented him ever having pleasure, and so on and so on. Slowly he came to recognize that what impeded him was an inner father. Later he substituted the term "inner tyrant" for father. It was moving when one day he said, "You know, I've suddenly realized my father must have had an inner tyrant too." I think in that moment he felt sad for his father and forgave him. I have no doubt that at that moment of forgiveness his own ego gained strength. What I am trying to get at is that the difference between splitting according to whole objects as opposed to part-objects is enormous. But it takes more emotional effort to achieve a splitting of part-objects.

> *Floor:* It's about the business of pain, and that it is very closely associated in most people's minds with evil, so you can very easily fall back into the whole business of good and evil and, within the concept, for instance, *The Zohar* concept of good being where everything is in its appropriate place and in the appropriate relation to everything else: it is almost natural to ask, what is the rightful place for *pain* in this? Somehow for most people it is very difficult to accept that there should be.

Yes, I do think it is quite important, which is why I said psychic pain is feeling guilt or feeling shame —it's just, I'm not sure even if the word pain is quite the right word, actually, because we associate pain with a physical type of thing; it's more like an anguish of spirit—I think that is a better term for what I am talking about. So it's not that you say, "It's *good* to go through this, my boy." It's that it is not avoidable. It is certainly one of the reasons why what makes it difficult for people to make a creative move is that they begin to *feel* these things then. A woman made a creative move forward at the age of 50, and she said, "I have wasted my whole life", and she said, "Well, it's too late now, there is no point in doing anything"—so I said, "Two things have happened: you have had an awful vision of the past plus a feeling that you have wasted your life, but now a decision has occurred, and you have said you are going to waste the *next* thirty years too." The one is not a necessary consequence of the other.

MEDITATION SEVEN

How our technique is affected by this outlook

I want to try to see how this approach alters the way one treats patients. The first thing to realize is that when you are speaking with a patient, the words are vehicles that carry an emotional message. Therefore, the actual mentality—mental state of the analyst or therapist—is the crucial factor. The healing factor is what one might call the benign meeting between two minds that come together. It is not essentially the words—it is the communication that's occurring between the emotional states of the two people. It has happened to me very often when supervising someone that they say, "I had such and such a thought, but, of course, I didn't say anything about it", and then it is quite clear from what follows that the patient has tuned into the therapist's thought. Maybe this is quite a good place to start—that if you have a thought and the thought has been generated from within the situation, you always need a good reason not to impart it. In other words, your medicine chest is made up of the thoughts that you have in the session. So if you ever find yourself saying, "Well, I had this thought, but I didn't say it or didn't act upon it", there may be reasons why you say to yourself "Well, I won't", but the burden is on you to explain why not. In other words, it is a bit like a doctor who has a medicine in his cupboard, and someone comes in with flu, and he's got the right medicine to hand out, but doesn't do so. He may have a reason for not doing so—that it might give the person pneumonia or something if he does—but the usual thing is that you have to ask why. I emphasize this because therapists often have a thought that they don't impart. If you link this with what I've said about creative communication, and then, your thoughts are not purely yours—they have arisen through the interaction between the two of you. You and a friend bake a cake together, and you eat the whole of it—not very generous. It is the meeting of healthy creative minds that is the curative factor.

The other thing I want to stress is that what brings about change is when there is inside the person a creative emotional act. It is quite important to get this, that it is not the interpretation—unless you understand the interpretation to include the inner emotional act that brings about change—but the inner emotional act itself that brings about change. Therefore I keep coming back to this: that if this structure is in place, one's job is to try to do something. I think I have tried to explain about how one has to try to tackle what I refer to as "the intensifiers", to enable the emotional act to occur. Now I'll just tell you a story that struck me acutely. A man was coming to see me, and he had had two analyses and some therapy, and he used to come in, and at the beginning of every session, he used to say: "You know, I am very guilty about sexual matters." It was rare for him to start a session without saying that. I thought to myself, "Well, one thing I can be quite certain of is that he knows he is quite guilty about sexual matters." However, one day he came in and said, "You know, the most extraordinary thing happened this morning. As I was shaving and looking at myself in the mirror, I suddenly realized that I am terribly guilty about sexual things", and I understood that he had had a real realization that came from inside himself. I also realized that the other statements were what he had been *told*. In his previous statement he had been disgorging himself of this irritating detritus within him. The words were the same in the two instances, but the emotional content was quite different. He invited me to make pronouncements. He was one of those people who would invite one to make pronouncements of one sort or another—so much so, that if he said something and you said anything to elaborate it, he would immediately say, "Oh, so *that's* what you think, is it?" And so therapists had been erected into gods. But I do just want to stress this because it has struck me once or twice, when seeing one or two people, and I suddenly had the thought: "I don't think this person has ever had an inner realization." He would often say, "Oh, I *feel* this has been a very good treatment", but it didn't actually relate to what had happened. That is one aspect of it.

There is another thing that I think is technically important. You probably know the statement that Bion made, where he says, "There is guilt that is not experienced, pain that's not suffered"; it seems to me that that is a very important statement, because it means normally people have the idea that there is no guilt unless you feel it: "I don't *feel* any guilt therefore it's not there" or "I don't *feel* any pain therefore it's not there." Bion's formulation in the grid is that it *is* there, but in a different form. Now getting back to not getting oneself into the position of God where you are giving an instruction: imagine, for instance, that a patient has a rather upsetting session, and then they don't turn up to the following one. It makes a very big difference if you say to the person, "I think you are defending yourself against anger towards me", as opposed to saying, "I think this is the way the anger manifests itself inside you." These are two quite different statements, because one is descriptive and the other implies that the patient is doing things wrongly. Say someone withdraws, and you say, "I think you are withdrawing because you are defending yourself against anger" that is quite a different statement from saying "I think this is the way anger 'talks' in you." In other words, it is an attempt to describe. As soon as you talk about the person defending themselves against it, you are saying, "There is a better way of expressing anger than that." Again, you override the possibility of the person themselves having an inner movement and realization that indicates change.

I can think of quite a well-known analyst with whom I was once discussing this issue of the way in which patients adopt and mimic the mental attitude and outlook of the analyst. This analyst said, "Oh, well, it's just one of those things that can't be helped"—but, you see, that is a completely different attitude, and one with which I totally disagree. It seems to me that if you take that view, then a person doesn't have an inner moment of realization or emotional understanding *or* a response to conscience. A lot of therapeutic endeavour is done on the basis that "This is the right way to be, you know, and this is the right way to express anger, to actually speak it etc., and you're not doing it right, my boy, this is the right way to be doing it and especially to be doing it the way *I* do it because *no one* does it better than I do it." I am exaggerating, but it's not possible, if you look at the psychoanalytic world, to avoid the conclusion that people are in submission to the point of view of another. There is a hypnotic function at work here. It is a question of values: do you think and feel that a person's freedom and their own inner free choice is something that you put value on, or not.

Part of the problem with this narcissistic type of constellation is that it only works if you hide it. There is *shame* about this whole constellation, and *guilt* about it, that has to be hidden. In nature there is the idea of mimicry. If birds eat a Monarch butterfly, it's bitter, and so they avoid eating it. Other moths that aren't Monarchs are, instead, mimics: they just look like Monarchs. Obviously the idea is that birds will think they are Monarchs, so they don't eat them. There is a spider that mimics ants and an ordinary fly that mimics a bee, and there are others as well. There is also mimicry of the genuine ones: hope, initiative, freedom, choice, person, giving, faith; and then you have the mimics. What may *look* like hope, is actually excitement; it may *look* like initiative, but it is actually impulsiveness; it may look like freedom, but it is in fact licence—it is not in a creative act; it *looks* like choice, but it's not, it is rationalization; and it looks like a person, but it's not, it's a hypocrite—a hypocrite in the sense of it being actually a type of *fake* person.

I have been quite struck by the fact that I have had a lot of patients who have said to me at some point or another, "I feel a fraud" or "I feel phoney" or "I feel an impostor"—those sorts of statements. I try to give an explanation of that in my paper "I Feel a Fraud" (see Appendix D). It is a sign that this constellation is in operation, but what it refers to is that the person hasn't had an act of understanding. They have ingested things, but without an act of understanding. It may refer to their profession, it may refer to their status, it can refer to quite a lot of different things, but I think it nearly always comes down to there not being an inner act of understanding, a creative act, and the person feels phoney. I give actually a personal example in that paper. I did psychology rather late in life, and I had at one point to do an exam on some aspects of experimental psychology. I put a hot towel around my head about 48 hours before the exam, and I learnt numerous experiments, including the names of the people who had done the experiments—there were always four names, and they were nearly always hyphenated—and I managed to commit them to memory. I had once read a book on how to develop a super-power memory, and I committed all this to my mind, and I went into the exam, and did my worst. I did quite well in the exam, and the examiner marking the paper probably thought, "Well, this fellow obviously knows his stuff"—but what he didn't know was that a week later the whole lot had disappeared out of my mind! There had been no act of understanding. That's what I am really getting at; it wasn't cheating technically, but it was psychologically.

And so then we have giving, and the mimic is prodigality. And the last one is rather important: faith as opposed to magic, and I think I prefer to leave you in a way to just think about those. The other one that I have put quite a lot of stress on is activity, what I have referred to as contemplation, and it is very important to realize that this doesn't mean a lot of movement that can look like activity though it isn't activity in the form that I'm talking about. If we go back to that article of Didier Houzel's and that therapist who sat there observing, he was exceedingly active, but it may not *look* like that. You also get that the difference really lies between the inner and how the thing looks on the outside.

What I would like to stress is that an interpretation always bring conscience into play. In fact, I think one could posit that it is the defining element in interpretation. What occurs in the space between an interpretation and a psychic move? It is that the person has responded to conscience, and conscience is the basis of religion—the sort of religion where I have spoken about the infinite or the absolute as being the ground in which we are all inserted. I might just give one example of this. There was a man who said his young daughter had been behaving in a dreadful way, and he had been in the middle of drafting an important letter on his computer when she had rushed in and turned it off. Then, in a rushed aside, he mentioned he wouldn't be here on Thursday to see me, so, from previous knowledge, it seemed clear that he was in a particular kind of mental state, which we had come to call the "tortoiseshell state". So I said to him that it seemed he was in this "tortoiseshell state", and then he said, "Ah, but I am always like that", which I knew was untrue, which I said and instanced occasions when he was not like that. When someone is in an intense state, its presence dominates all other states of mind, which are then obliterated. I was eroding the dogmatism of the state.

I think the important point here was my own intuition, which I decided to stand by rather than be bulldozed by his dogmatism, and therefore what he met at that moment was me as a person standing by my own intuition, my own memory of other states he was in, and my own *certainty* that he was not always critical, but that he was when he was in this "tortoiseshell state". It is personal certainty—NOT dogmatism—which dissolves the rigidity of a psychotic state. The end of that story was that when he went home, he found that his daughter was in a much better state, and this was, I believe, because he had come out of the "tortoiseshell state". His meeting me as a person dissolved the shell of the tortoise. As this is important, I shall give two more examples.

I said to this chap, "You haven't said this before", and he said "Oh yes I did, I did once say it before." He said, "You quite often forget things", so I said to him "That's quite an important piece of information then that you have, that I quite often forget things, because it now means that you must then say to yourself when anything is important, 'I must drum this into Neville's head because he often forgets things'." This perception of me means he now has to bring forth something out of himself. Of course, what he says to himself is "Therapists *shouldn't* ever forget anything", but that's some totally imaginary figure. He would like it to be like that because then he could stay put in his passive state—he can remain a jelly.

I'll give you another example: A woman said, "I've noticed sometimes I bring something up, and you don't always follow it through"; so I said exactly the same to her—I said, "You now have a bit of knowledge here and so you need to drum this into my head." The naked fact of my personhood demands that she be a person too. Reality confronts her and me. The man who was a chap of considerable integrity and honesty subsequently said, "It's not only you, I have noticed I don't say things clearly enough to other people either"—so he followed it up with a personal realization about himself. Subsequently he began to say what he thought more clearly. So people began to think "Ah, so *that's* what he thinks", whereas before they didn't know that, you see. They began to see a person.

> *Floor:* You mentioned that realization happens when the person emotionally responds to conscience, and also conscience being the basis of religion. Can you talk a little bit more about conscience?

My paper, a rather dry academic type of paper, but I said it's an exegesis of the way Freud uses the word conscience. I'll tell you how I came to write it. An analyst colleague said, "Oh, conscience is the same as the superego", and that's what made me go and do this exegesis on Freud. The point really is that Freud had the same view that St Paul had, of conscience really being like a punishing God. But conscience in King David was not like that actually—when the prophet Nathan came to him and said, "You are the man", it touched his conscience, and he said "I've sinned against Yahweh." At the Enlightenment—and I think it was due to the collapse, or partial collapse of traditional religion and Christendom in Europe—conscience came into play again, and it had a much greater role, for instance, within Protestantism than within Catholicism. People like Rousseau put conscience very much at the centre of things, but their understanding of it was like something that is an invitation from within. It is *not* a castigation; it is an invitation, and so it is slightly difficult to try to grasp this, but the following of conscience is a free act. It is not put as an obligation—"You must do it"—it comes as an inner invitation. There is this terrific resistance in people to avoid it, and "If I can get someone else to tell me to do this, I probably will." It comes back to that picture of the *Baptism of Christ* by Piero della Francesca; as soon as there is a moment like that and conscience is followed, it does mean that there is an inner anointing. It puts responsibilities upon the person. It's a burden, it brings suffering, it brings anguish—all the things that, as Bion said, we like to evade.

> *Floor:* Just a rider, really: I think the root of the word in its original use meant consciousness, and in Shakespeare and Elizabethan literature conscience does mean consciousness—

"Conscience doth make cowards of us all", Hamlet is talking about consciousness, and I think that illustrates what you are talking about.

Yes, that is right, and I think it does for a particular reason: because something only becomes conscious when you act. You only become aware of things when you freely act. One of the things Isaiah Berlin emphasizes in his exegesis of the philosopher Vico is that Vico said, "Actually, you only really know what you create." Therefore Vico said that you know the things that come from within and what you create *better* than external things, which are totally outside your own creation. This was in contradiction to Descartes and the Enlightenment, which held that the external world is known better. Vico was a believer in a God who created, and therefore he said that God knew *because* he created, but he used that same sort of analogy. It was to me the most illuminating moment when I read that, because I thought "My heavens", if this is so and the whole of psychoanalysis is concerned with bringing things to awareness, and if Vico is right that awareness only happens when you create, then it throws a different light on how you bring things into awareness. Actually, neither one's positive assets come into awareness nor the negative ones, because the negative only comes into focus when it gets silhouetted against the positive, and it's one of the reasons why people are very fearful of making a creative step. In my view that alters in a profound way the way one sees the psychoanalytic endeavour. Freely responding to conscience is also a creative act, and therefore the development of virtue is a precondition also for the development of awareness, of consciousness.

Floor: I found very interesting especially the narcissistic constellation and how when you mentioned in several examples that when you got into a less Godly-like place, the patient would respond. Now I would be very interested to hear how you deal with the resistance in the patient that then comes and doesn't *want* that less Godly-like relationship, wants to keep in place you as the Godly-like therapist. Is it repetition of the same statements—I mean, can you say a bit more on that?

Well one has to think that's why (see frontispiece) you see; what's very important with this is that the person may want what they have come for because they are suffering in some way, and there'll be some other aspect of this that they don't want. What they may not realize is that if they don't want to be exploited and put down and so on and be worm-like, then the god has to be transformed. So although the person may be resistant to giving up their god, you can tackle it somewhere else. What is manifested may be complaints about how exploited they are and how they can never get anywhere in their job, how people are always unpleasant to them, or whatever the actual story is: you will know when you hear these things that you are being erected into a god. The fact that you are being erected into a god is a very important part of the system and it can be tackled, but it's important to realize that the whole lot is an interrelating system, so if you start from the point of the patient's complaint, it will lead back to the god in such a way that the patient can see its damaging effects. If we had bigger minds we could see this was one thing—although at any one moment we cannot *see* that it is, but we can *know* it.

Floor: So that's basically staying in that contemplative as well—a bit of a contemplation state?

The other quite important thing that I have noticed is quite odd: that somehow there is so much therapeutic work done what I call on the surface. Let's say a patient says, "I know I am very obstinate when I meet up with someone that's trying to explain something to me", and at a later point, when he is being resistant, you can say, "But, listen, you've *told* me you are very obstinate, and I think this is an instance of it." I don't mean you have to be a passive wallflower—you can use something you've been *told*. They may have told you a year before; that doesn't matter—you can now bring it up; but therapists often think, "It's just this interaction", and the fact that something was said to you a year before outlaws you from using it. Well, why not use it? If you are in an ordinary conversation with someone, you bring up things from the past, or things that people have said, etc. So I don't want to make it sound as if one's just there in some passive mode, but it is quite different if someone has *told* you something, *they've* told you this, and they *know* such and such, and if there is a good interpretation, the person will often say, "Yes, I *know* I am very shy about doing such and such" or "I *know* I am far too assertive and bullying over such and such." You can say you *know* this, you see.

> *Floor:* It's extremely stimulating but also challenging for me, a psychoanalyst, who has worked for many years. I think change is very difficult because there are some points—many points, in fact—which very much make me think about changes in my technique. Yesterday you spoke about not using the word to the patient, not speaking; you *feel* this way, and this is very important. For instance, I have a habit, a routine, speaking so, and now I thought the whole time about one of my most difficult patients who, I think, is on the verge of breaking off with analysis and who is always silent, and he told me all over again, "Well, I don't want you to tell me what *I* feel, I want you to tell me what *you* feel, how you are involved." For the whole time I thought about it—I am Kleinian tradition—of this man being envious of me—he's also in the helping professions—wanting to make me small, to speak about me, but now I start thinking that there was something totally wrong in our interaction that I don't understand, but I think I have a hint of it. Could you tell me something about it?

Well, I think you are right; I don't know how to answer that, exactly. But I think the patient is right about something, which is that he or she is wanting something from you. If you go back to the point about the extreme negativity that's in there anyway, especially in a very disturbed patient, there is a very powerful type of negativity, so my guess is that if you are talking about envy and so on, it doesn't get to where it is. I think it must somehow mean that the patient is wanting some understanding from you of something different. The only example I can give is in my book *The Analytic Experience*. I have been through exactly this sort of journey, in a way, but it was a long time ago. I was seeing a woman, and she was terrifically attacking, and I went on and on about the envy and undermining and this and that and the other, and certain people would have been proud of me, but this poor woman went back to a counsellor who had originally referred her, and the counsellor said, "I don't think he can hear a baby screaming." She came back and she said this, and I thought "My God, she's right", and suddenly I could hear a whole different register, and she had gone and come back and forced this into my head. So when she said that, I just said, "I think that's totally correct", and she burst into tears. So, what I am trying to get at is if you go back to the idea of the trauma—this whole situation *is* the trauma, it has been generated by the trauma. I think it relates a bit to what I was saying that if a patient does definitely tell one certain things, and they know certain things you can begin to build up a picture of actually what the distress is here. If you can remember that envy is something that is defined by what I refer to as the bee sting that I get stung by, as it were, and what actually is it, though, inside the person. When I am stung by a bee, I only feel the sting—it does not tell me the structure of the bee itself. I think if one can get oneself into that sort of mental register, then the situation can begin to change.

I'll just tell you one other story with a woman that I was seeing. She, again, was very attacking and sadistic and kept on saying things to me like "There's something you don't understand", but with terrific hostility. It so happened that many years ago, when Bion used to come across from America and take supervision, I took this woman to him for supervision, and so I explained to him how I thought she was trying to get something true across to me, but also that it was done in a very sadistic way. He just said, in the nicest possible way, "It's a very strange thing, you know, but sadism only works if the victim is helpless." So, you understand what I mean. It's the thing I have been trying to say in another way: if one responds differently, it is no longer sadism.

MEDITATION EIGHT

The spirit of sanity: discussion of central issues

Floor: I was very interested in what you said about the patient who said something about how she was always obstinate, and you said "You've often told me about that, your obstinacy." I was relieved to hear you saying that because sometimes if I make that sort of comment about something they have told me in the past, I find myself thinking about Bion's edict about going to a session without memory and desire. I wondered if you could comment on that.

Whenever you go for supervision, the same principle applies as in analysis: that if you have some understanding as a result of the supervision that will help you, then good, but I tell supervisees to say to themselves when they leave, "Fuck Neville Symington!" Push him out of your mind and get on with it, and you must do the same with Bion, I am afraid. He is trying to convey something, and what he meant was that you mustn't go into a session thinking "I must remember what the patient said." Say, the patient is speaking about something, and you *remember* what they've told you. If you've got an active memory and it is stimulated, you remember naturally—it isn't generated from some anxious state. Bion said, in fact, that if you are sort of in a state anxious to *forget*, that is not right either. He's trying to get across that it needs to come spontaneously. So if the patient is speaking and perhaps in a rebellious type mode, then you remember that "Of course, he *told* me that he's very obstinate", and you can say, "Look, you've *told* me this"—but it's not because you've written it on a pad, and said "I must remember this as I go into the session." But I still take that first point too, that you mustn't have edicts around if you can help it.

> *Floor:* There are lots of people who are interested about this meeting of religion and psychotherapy. There is this question: could these fields come together, could they cooperate? I definitely think they are both very important for me, but this is one question. The other question is, do religions need experience from within the psychotherapy field and the other way around? The religion that I am close to is Orthodox Christianity, which I didn't hear you mentioning during this conference, and which I think could be very important for all of that. Probably people from this field would say, "No we don't." I spoke with a monk once, and I definitely understand it because there is so [much] fullness of experience within this field, although I do believe there is very important thing in psychotherapy. For me, if I look as a psychotherapist, there is a lot of need for something from the field of religion—like basic values. The other thing is what we are called for.

Do you mind if I stop you there? Is there anything else that you want to add to that?

> *Floor:* I am actually trying to develop something.

OK, all right.

> *Floor:* I will shorten this now. Basically, if we look at a basic concept in psychoanalysis—and I think psychoanalysis had been developing in the context of positivistic–scientific model at that time, but I don't think it is basically much changed, although there are lots of developments. I am just asking myself, and I would like to ask you what you think this

framework could allow for concepts from different religious frameworks. I would think that the psychoanalytic basic framework is far too narrow to really allow for that. This is kind of a question, not a statement, really.

In my book on *Emotion and Spirit* one of the main points I try to make is that what I refer to as the core values of religion are needed, but the traditional religions have not got a good hold on the way the emotions work. That has been particularly the preserve of psychoanalysis and the therapies that derive from it; and then also, psychoanalysis requires the psychological understanding that has come from the great religions, so that's one point. I didn't understand the point you made about Christianity.

> *Floor:* My final point is: could the basic concepts—when we really look into basic concepts of psychoanalysis—could they allow for acceptance or something which I think is a much wider concept of religious concepts?

I think if you bring any two things like this into connection with one another, each has to give up something, but also each can become enriched. Now, to me there are certain problems. It seems to me that certain things about the teaching of Jesus and the emphasis on the inner, the role of suffering and its capacity to transform, all these things seem to me to be very important. However, I think, for instance, I would find it very difficult as a psychoanalyst looking at that to assert the divinity of Christ, say. That's a difficult one, because it's a very central type of doctrine for Christians. It may sound a rather disagreeable thing to say, but I do think that there is such a crisis in the sphere of values in the world that it is necessary for *all* the great religions to think "Well, we may be wrong about something here."

> *Floor:* Like what?

For instance, take, say, the doctrine of the divinity of Christ, or, for instance, say, within Catholicism, the doctrine of transubstantiation. I feel ok about speaking about this because I was brought up within the Roman Catholic field, so I feel that I can say that. But I think in all the religions you can actually point to things that seem to have perverted its central message. I've tried to say something about that in terms of Judaism and the birth of conscience, which was a genius of insight in the people, but it does mean that you keep getting this interplay between an amazing spiritual insight on one side versus a divinization on the other. So it seems to me that all the religions need to consider their true riches and be prepared to change their way of thinking about some of the other aspects.

> *Floor:* I just wondered whether you feel there is room for a complementary view to that . . .

How do you mean?

> *Floor:* Well, just answering that last point: can it be opened up to discussion, I feel that's something . . .

No, no, I certainly think it needs to be open for discussion, and the other thing that probably needs to occur is that whenever two things come together I think you get a better view of what's actually essential and what's the inner moving spirit, both of psychoanalysis and of different religions.

> *Floor:* I must say first of all that I greatly value practically everything that Neville says, but on this last point I feel a rather different viewpoint might add something, because, you see, we all see these large problems in our own way, and I feel he is wrong when he says the churches must have a fresh look at their theology. I don't think that is *possible*, and I don't think it is helpful to say it. I think it is much better if we think in terms of the evolution of consciousness. Now we are on the Internet, we have an incredible opportunity of exchanging views. People have been thinking about this in rather different ways—for example, there is a book called *The Symmetry of God* by my friend Rodney Bomford, in which he really, in a controversial way, writes about Christianity as *myth*. He is a parish priest, and nobody is going to question his motives or his practice, but he is able to think, following Mircea Eliade, in terms of Christianity as myth. Well, I found that interesting. It's not what I do. I have covered it from a different angle and I have written a book called *Midwifery of the Soul*, which is the history of my twenty-year struggle to put together my psycho-

analytic knowledge and the fact that I have faith. Neville is an enormous help to me, because I see him struggling with his faith and how to be a person and so forth, having pushed away the doctrines of the Roman Catholic Church. I think what would be much more useful to say—and you haven't actually said this, I don't think, Neville—but when you look at that picture, that is what happens to religions. It happens to organized religion, and it happens to any spiritual insight that anybody has—it gets organized into a narcissistic system. Church has become political, so what we have to do is evolve, and what we need is more people—I think there are increasing numbers of them about—who can think about more than one religion at a time. This is what I have been doing—entirely on my own, I may say, just by reading—and it develops one's understanding.

Well, I agree with that. I did say actually at the outset that I thought that about Eastern religions as opposed to the Judaeo–Christian tradition, that it seems to me that that notion of the absolute, for instance, that *is* existence, has been understood in the East, but that the personal has been particularly elucidated within the Judaeo–Christian. I am in agreement with that. There is a problem though, which I'll try to just describe in a different way. It's the sort of problem that I tried to talk about with Meissner, where it seems he is in a philosophical position in that determinist type of position *and* at the same time trying to marry up psychoanalysis with his Christian faith, but it requires him to relinquish the determinist philosophy on one side and a fideism on the other. It is not actually a proper union that has taken place. It is very odd because he hasn't got a religious philosophy there when he is thinking about psychoanalysis, so he is trying to marry two things that actually don't fit. It's not coherent.

Floor: I absolutely do agree with that, but you have reminded me of the thing I really objected to, which was when you said religions don't understand the emotions. The way parish priests go around enquiring why young couples haven't had babies is obviously a dreadful thing to happen, but what I find so dismal, because I am getting old and I can remember

> a different world, is that people have *lost* the understanding that comes. There is enormous understanding in all religions, that's what they are about—how shall we live?—you know, and that's what worries me, frankly, about your approach—that you push things away, whereas every religion—and all the people I have spoken to here are interested in this, one has to be—the point about holistic thinking that the absolute, the infinite, which is what I go back to the Middle Ages for my understanding through Christianity, and that you have to be inclusive; it's all about integration as opposed to fragmentation. We mustn't push things away.

Yes, I understand that, but do you think though that in the religious traditions those very primitive emotional activities are well understood?

> *Floor:* Oh, yes, and if you read Bonford he is very good on this, because all the myths are precisely about this. I've personally done a lot about mythology around the world—all the creation myths have something equivalent to the Garden of Eden and the Fall of Man, and this is the fascinating question: what is it about being human that makes us feel guilty, and how do we cope with the problem of guilt? I had a phase when I thought that Matthew Fox had the answer, but I am not so sure about that now. If you think about original blessing instead of original sin, it is something you can actually chew over. I haven't got any answers, but *that* is the essential question. I am absolutely with you when you talk about getting the person, the act of faith, I mean, I think you know a lot about it, and it resonates with me.

Do you think, though, that psychoanalysis has brought any new knowledge about the way the emotions operate?

> *Floor:* Well, of course I do, yes.

But that's what I mean, you see.

> *Floor:* But it's another kind of theology, and how to integrate the two is the task for the next millennium, isn't it—how do we

put these things together? Not by chucking out things we don't like, because the punitive stuff is bound to come, and people want rules. The other thing about what you were saying about how important it is that people push away the opportunity to be a person—they are scared stiff, as you say. We all believe in human rights and equality and democracy and giving people opportunities. How do we deal with the fact a lot of people do not *want* to become people and think for themselves?

Ok, now, I think I should take one or two of the people who put their hands up initially, and I'll try to pick one or two people who haven't spoken. Bernadine Bishop?

> *Floor:* I am rather abandoning the question I wanted to ask originally if that's all right in order to say something about the absolutely gripping debate which is evolving at the moment, because just following on from what I think Margaret Arden has just been saying and what was in the room in fact about all of this, where some of us *do* feel that religion does understand the fundamentals of human emotional experience. I think that one of the reasons why religions are accused, shall we say, of *not* having understood emotional experience is that emotional experience has never been *central* to religious understandings. Religion is in the pursuit of something else, pursuit of the infinite, the absolute, the love of God or whatever we want to call it in different generations. So the understanding of human emotions tends to be tangential to that. It is something that happens, so yes, what could be more fundamental and understanding of primal envy than the murder of Christ? I mean, I think it is all there, it's just that it's not central.

> *Floor* [Isca]: I don't accept that at all.

> *Floor* [Bernadine]: Would you like to answer that, then?

> *Floor* [Isca]: No I wouldn't, but I just don't agree with that, that it's a question of envy, but a question of really humanizing God, which was not acceptable to Judaism? Buddhism— it was something of an ultimate reality.

136   THE SPIRIT OF SANITY

> *Floor* [Bernadine]:   Why shouldn't that be understood as envy?
>
> *Floor* [Isca]:   Why *should* it be understood as envy?
>
> *Floor* [Margaret]:   Well, if you'll forgive me, Isca, that's as much as to say that Jews didn't suffer from envy. I'm saying that that's the implication of what you say.
>
> *Floor* [Isca]:   . . . you have many different views of that, but you put it down as an *absolute*.
>
> *Floor* [Margaret]:   No, no, it's a point of view. I agree with you, Bernadine, one has to keep these things in play.
>
> *Floor* [Bernadine]:   . . . why what I said has incurred so much response.
>
> *Floor* [Isca]:   Well, I am just saying that there may be other views.
>
> *Floor* [Bernadine]:   Why should it sound as if I am speaking from the podium?

I think I'll take another question. It's that I've found quite often if one takes another question, then one can go on thinking. Someone here called Karen Young, who I don't think has spoken.

> *Floor:* My question isn't related to this. The question that I have is about the state of contemplation that you talked about, and how you talked particularly about a patient whom you experienced as angry, and you felt irritated by the lady who felt she had got some understanding from her gynaecologist and were able to make a deeper understanding than reflecting back some of her anger. I wondered how, being at the beginning of the struggle of trying to be a therapist, where that comes in, and how in your religious life, in one's inner spiritual life, how that can enable, in fact, talking about this link between, I am actually also trying to struggle with my religious beliefs and my practice as a therapist.

I'll try to answer this in this way. You see, that was a clear case where what she said was put in a sticky envelope, as it were, but it was only sticky to the extent to which my self-esteem—"I had been doing very good work, you know, and I don't want this to be criticized"—that is what she tickled, as it were. She tickled something of this in me. Now I'll just perhaps tell you a story. When I started to write on psychoanalysis and religion, I said to myself, "the key linking concept is narcissism". All the great religious teachers, what they were on about was to try to help liberate people from their narcissistic state. It also then struck me that there was a mass of literature within psychoanalysis and within psychotherapy on narcissism and narcissistic patients, and so on, so obviously this was something that analysts were saying needed to be tackled. So it struck me therefore that this must be the link between psychoanalysis and religion. And then I scratched my head and said, "Well, what *is* narcissism?" So I set myself the task of trying to understand what it was and is and I am *still* trying to understand it, and that's sort of part of the journey. But, you see, I don't think there is any conflict between that and a spiritual endeavour, because that actually is what all the great religious teachers were on about. In one way and another they were trying to liberate people from this system. I don't really mind how you put it, but you might put it this way—that with that woman, when I was being stimulated in that way, and she was tickling me, I don't mind whether you say it was Jesus, or King David, or one of the prophets, or Buddha, or one of the seers of the Upanishads, as it were, put their hand on my shoulder and said, "Just calm down, Symington, listen to her."

I think I'd better just take someone called Rosemary Malcolm?

Floor: My question is about pushing away the opportunity to be a person. I was thinking about the difficulty of my own kind of transference reaction which can be irritation: "Oh, my stars, here we go again", when somebody who is not wanting to grow up makes progress, makes progress, and then suddenly has an opportunity to do something and says, "I hear a little voice saying don't do that, don't do that." I wondered if you could say a bit more about technique there.

Could you say a little bit more, I haven't quite understood . . .

Floor: My own irritation with the blocks that are put in the way.

Right, ok, well, I think the really difficult thing, for which there is no solution, is if you are not aware that you are irritated. That's the real problem. But if you are aware and there's a sense [that] "This person's getting under my skin" type of thing, I think what is necessary then is attention—one's psychic attention needs to be turned from there to there. You turn it to yourself. The technical problem then is how do you act and operate, but the task is to try to process. When you are in a flared-up state, you don't get understanding. I have had so many instances of it—it is at the moment when it begins to calm that insight comes. I had a man once who was terrifically provocative, and several times we got into a wrangle. I knew that this was no good, so I said to him, "You know, if there was someone sitting over there in that chair and looking at the two of us, they would see that something had gone wrong here, and that we had got into a mess", and that calmed the atmosphere—a sort of third presence was brought in. So I can't exactly tell you, but you have to do something to start to contain the state that you are in, and as soon as you do, the thing changes. Understanding partners tranquillity; agitation breeds confusion.

> *Floor:* I wonder if you could say something about the loss of the structure that the old religions have provided within society, because I think that was where we were with that discussion a bit. I think people are saying, can we integrate the old religions into psychoanalytic thought. I can see that we can integrate it into our practice on a one-to-one basis, but the fact is that we might choose to go back to Christianity or Judaism, but we are, most of us, are middle-aged, and I think society is evolving in a different way, more in the way that you've been talking about. I think what you've been talking about is the new religion. I've been working on it myself for thirty years and have been left feeling in a state of chaos and loneliness, and I am sure I am not alone—and I think our children are not going to go back to Christianity, or church, or . . .

Yes, I think you are very largely right. That's why I gave the example of when my wife and I went to the lecture by this American teacher who experienced a terrific collapse of values on returning to visit some schools in America. She felt pushed towards some fundamentalist solution, but she was too sensible and realized that wasn't the solution but knew that there were some types of religious values required. I suppose what the answer must be is that there is a big pressure on the traditional religions to change their form, so their ways of seeing and understanding things change— even, it seems to me on the question of conscience. For instance, when you think of the intricate problems that are now thrown up by medical ethics—say, in terms of euthanasia and all the intricate problems of *in vitro* fertilization, surrogate motherhood etc.—I personally think there will be a much greater pressure put on all traditional religions to help people clarify the content of their consciences. I just don't think you can legislate for everything like this; there are new developments the whole time. Traditional religions have far too much tended to lay down "This is what you should do", and "sex is all right between two people who are married and have been through a ceremony", and "Death must only occur under certain circumstances", etc., but I think because of the intricacy and the quick changingness the type of respect for individual freedom and helping people to clarify their consciences will become much, much more important. I'd have thought the traditional religions will need to push in that direction, and I think it will probably mean quite considerable changes in their outlook and structure.

> *Floor:* I was thinking that just as narcissism is one of the sort of over-arching connections between analysis and religion, so is contemplation. It almost seems to me that contemplation is at the heart of what is in common with all the major religions— the sense of amazement and awe and wonder, that fertility of creation and the extraordinariness of it all, and that when one is in a narcissistic state one can't contemplate anything, because one's too involved internally.

Yes, yes, I think that is true.

> *Floor:* If you are projecting from inside you onto other things, you can't see what's there, and I think that is connected with the idea of conscience. Also, it struck me when this lady was talking about conscience that the Latin derivation is "knowing with", and that it is something that develops in that contemplative act that you were describing between the mother

and the infant—that was a loving recognition of who you are, that's how you develop a conscience, as well as a whole self, and that this pattern that you have described so vividly is the index of a disaster.

Yes, I think that's right.

Floor: And that when people come to therapy or analysis in this state, what we are trying to do is salvage something from the disaster by enabling the jelly to turn into protoplasm, almost, and to emerge as a person.

Yes, I think that is a very valuable contribution. I hadn't ever actually quite thought that contemplation is a linking point, but I am sure that is correct.

Floor: You may have touched on it already, but I wondered if you could say a little bit more—if you could extend your thoughts around conscience to the group, to the social, how the voice of conscience is smothered or respected in the wider social organizational society.

Yes, that's a difficult one, really, isn't it. It reminds me of Bion's thing of The Mystic in the Group. Well, just to go back, you know, to that point I've made a couple of times: that if you have a thought and you voice it and that is something that is echoed and felt by others in the group, there clearly is an interaction between the group in which there is a pressure to conform to a particular way, and against something creative, as opposed to something else that's also in the group. But I think more is located within the individual than is required to be spoken, and that can have a leavening effect in the group. It is one of the reasons why I said in terms of technique that if the analyst has a thought, he has to question himself if he doesn't impart it. That's number one. But it is also in a group situation that one needs to ask oneself the same question. I have been in group situations where, perhaps on a committee or something, I have had both experiences, where I have come away and said, "You're a coward because you didn't speak really what you thought", and other times when I *haven't* been and I *have* spoken what I've thought, and nearly always when you do speak what you think, say, that's something guided by conscience or one's own free act, it does have some leavening effect. It may be contradicted, and there is an actual growth that comes out of it.

> *Floor:* Could I just make the connection with silences—that where there is a silence in a group or in society, there is conscience being smothered.

Well, it depends, because there are silences that are peaceful.

> *Floor:* I don't mean a contemplative silence—I mean the silence where something is unspoken because it is not conscious, but not necessarily conscious, but there is a deep silence.

I think what you are saying there is the smothering, as it were, the much more powerful smothering is the more primitive non-verbal pressure; that is what Melanie Klein called projective identification—it's that sense of strong group pressure which actually smothers. Nothing is said, but there is a pressure not to speak—that's one of the reasons that in psychotherapy and psychoanalysis it is so important that if someone has a problem about speaking in the face of someone who is disapproving, that's a problem and one to be worked with, and hopefully the person will develop a greater capacity to be able to so that they'll actually function in the group, not only with the individual but also within a group, in a way that is leavening to the group. Otherwise these criticisms often made against psychoanalysis that it just accommodates people to the establishment are true, unless one looks at it in this other way.

> *Floor:* What I've been thinking about all the way through, and it has now been spoken about a bit, is how we bring up our children, and connecting that with—I suppose I think psychoanalysis addresses what's within, but the traditional religions—well, maybe not so much Buddhism—talk about the God out there as well and how this alters our thinking, this idea of a God out there. I was very much struck by what you said at the beginning about the teacher who went back to America and what's happened to our society, and I sort of wonder whether what has happened is connected to the lack of an idea of a God out there—whether that's right or wrong, I don't know—and an additional parental figure, if you like,

and I don't think the idea of a God out there needs to detract from what happens inside. I was brought up a Catholic, and there was a great emphasis on prayer—what we were talking about, contemplation—and on examining one's own conscience in the Cardinal Newman sense—the emphasis on what you think and feel yourself is more important than what the Pope says, but I sort of feel that that idea of stopping and thinking, examining your conscience, prayer, not acting on impulse—that's what has gone from the world, or is dying in the world, I think.

Yes, I think that is probably true. Just to correct one thing, though, all the great religions have what one might call a folk-religion type of aspect to them and then a deeper spiritual aspect. In the deeper spiritual understanding in all the great religions the idea of the divine is internal, there is no doubt about that, and someone was speaking to me about St Augustine earlier, where he says: "I looked for God here, there, and everywhere, and finally I looked within, and that's where I found Him." So I just want to sort of correct that. I don't really think that the idea of a benign type of paternal presence that is watching over one kindly is a very helpful thing, really. I think it's . . . to me, it's part of this system, really. I think it's the internal that's the genuine article.

Jonathan, you haven't asked a question yet, have you, and I know . . .

Floor: I just wanted to make a brief comment. It connects with a thought that Pat Land mentioned earlier and linking to your very first talk about "An Ontology for Sanity". I was looking at this interesting diagram, and I am wondering what elements would go towards an ontology for sanity and what would be the effect. It seems to me that one issue that would need to develop would be that of permeability, and I just wondered if you had any thoughts about the fluidity of the model, if you like, and what the inside would look like through this process of connecting tissues, really, in connection with the outside and the inside in quite a dynamic way.

One thing I think needs to be said, and I think my book on narcissism is defective in this way, is that one needs to see it as a current in all of us that can become more dominating or less dominating and that therefore it is fluid in that sense. I think it is quite important in that if it's tremendously dominating, that's all you sort of meet, and then you think the whole person is just that, and it's quite important. I always think an important bridge has been crossed in therapy or analysis at the moment when the person is able to see that there is a monster in them and, as it were, a healthy striving, and they can see it within rather than projected out. So what I am trying to get at is that it is clearly fluid. I would just like to stress the other thing—that is, I don't think it is got rid of, it's *transformed* so that it becomes an asset to the personality rather than something that is dysfunctional.

> *Floor:* In that transformation that you are saying this persona has, a thought came to me in relation to each interpretation we make, that it might have its own narcissistic constellation, on its own. How, if you try, it can be seen in a global way, but it can also be seen that sometimes it might work with a patient one moment, and you both get in contact to the real, and you get rid of the false or the Godly-like side of you, but the next moment you might regress back to that place it was before, so it's almost like a constant dynamic, even in a session.

That's true, yes, that's absolutely true.

> *Floor:* I just wanted to add a point to what Stella was saying, very quickly. You see, I think—I don't know, Stella, tell me if I've got it wrong—that Stella was saying that if one is bringing up children, then parents in relation to, say, adolescents have to be rebelled against, and that in order to do parenting is there a need for some outer figure that, if you like, is in addition to the parents. I see it almost as a sort of container, some image of a benign God that actually helps this process—you know, parents have a very difficult job. Was that what you were getting at, Stella?

> *Floor* (Stella): Yes, children internalize their parents' attributes, and I don't think it's *just* about a God out there, because I

mean I was brought up very much with the idea of a soul being there and God being in your soul, so it wasn't *just* out there, it's this feeling that children relate to something out there. I think all children have a bit of God in them as well, but it's really a question about *what* we tell our children. I think there's a lot of children who just know about religion as an academic subject, now, in schools; they are not brought up in any faith, and I question if that's a good thing, and whether they do learn to listen to themselves inside, and that's my question. I feel religions nurture that ability to reflect—or they *can* do.

No, no, they certainly can. What Pat Land said about contemplation has certainly fostered that.

I just want to come back to that debate that went on before. I think it's quite true—Aldous Huxley says that it is twentieth-century arrogance to think that there was no understanding of psychology and emotions before Freud, and it is clearly true. He quotes, for instance, some letters of Archbishop Fénelon, where he talks about the virtue of simplicity, which actually my wife, Joan, and I quoted in our book on Bion—letters that demonstrate remarkable understanding of inner emotions. But psychoanalysis has brought an understanding of things like the way different emotions interact inside the person—all the things that Freud talked about: displacement and condensation and so on, and if one thinks of Bion and his understanding of hallucinations and the way the subject takes in something and then expels it through the eyes, so that they see the image—there has been a great growth of understanding that wasn't within traditional religions. All my point in saying this is that the traditional religions do need to make use of this knowledge, *and* psychoanalysis needs those eternal truths derived from religion—that's the point I really wanted to make.

Floor: What I wanted to say is, when I hear the view about psychoanalysis and the institutionalized religion, I don't know, as a layman who is just interested and has no clinical experience, I feel that somehow there is a tendency always to seek new dogma, new instructions all the time. As you said earlier, people really like to be told what to do. Well, that goes against what is the sense of sanity, and the sense of religion to an extent. Now, institutionalized religions go through highs and lows. The values are there, and so far as psychoanalysis, the way I see it, is there as a method of investigation. There are all sorts of metaphors to represent how to do it. Your approach, which I think is enriching what has been a trend to forget, your motto . . . a question of misuse of language to a great extent, to an extent that soul, evil, almost become four-letter words not to be included in it. Well I think that what I always admired in your work is this question of redefining the value by the correct use of the words. It does not mean that if religions have arrived to excesses the values are no good, and it does not mean that in bringing up children one has to go and say "What is a religion? What are we going to tell them?" It is always up to us. The individual is part of society, so your approach, restating what is available, I think, creates a beautiful harmony, so why try to focus on certain specific items and why try to say "Well, yes that religion . . ."? I find no problem in your not accepting the divinity of Christ, not because I am a Jew, because that is easy enough because I never accepted it, but it is like in Judaism—there is always the eternal question between the written and the oral, which is a paradox in itself. But life *is* a paradox, and I think your attitude to always seek the correct definition, I think that is the key in a way, in agreement with Margaret Arden, that is how you *save to life* by having your bearing quite clear. Thank you.

I think the important thing is this—it's not even the question, for instance, of the divinity of Christ or other doctrines in other religions, I don't think that's quite the key. I think it's as soon as you split on the basis of this one being good and that one being bad, that's the problem. My difficulty with the divinity of Christ is that it tends to say, well, this one was perfect, you see. That has to mean the others are bad in some way or another. It is the same within Judaism, when, to my mind, I talk about the genius of the ancient Israelites through whom conscience came to birth, but I think it's mistaken as soon as you begin to get a God that specially chose this people, and I think that's a mistake because it robs the people of their creative spiritual genius and how they gave this to the world.

That's what I mean. I think it's tremendously important to split according to mentalities and not according to whole agglomerated institutions, whether it is a religion, whether it is a school of psychoanalysis, a political party, etc. It is much more work to do that, it's much easier to say, "This is good and that's bad" and "Labour's good, Tories are bad", that's quite easy to do.

> *Floor:* I guess I have a curiosity to know whether you have found that as you have made, or struggled to make, this integration and holding, I assume, I'm assuming, increasingly a presence which is open to seeing the person that you are working with in a much bigger context, including a spiritual one, and seeing them as emerging from this infinite and absolute, as you've said it. Has that influenced the kind of issues that are brought to you? Do you actually find yourself sitting with patients increasingly bringing issues of their relationship to the infinite and bringing spiritual concerns into their analysis with you? If so, do you have a nice juicy example? And how do you approach it?

I'm certainly very aware of when there is evidence of a struggle inside someone between a conscience that is beckoning them and some other sort of force. Certainly I am very aware of it. But I think perhaps the most important aspect which I have tried to stress is that the more it is possible for the person to be free, that to me is absolutely central, that a person has their *own* realization. It is quite complicated, this, because sometimes that realization will be helped and aided by the analyst being able to speak. You do get the opposite thing, where you know if you have been a smoker or something and you half know you shouldn't be because it's bad for your lungs, and then you go to a doctor, and the doctor says, "You really must stop, you know"—it makes an impact, and you realize something. In the same way that can happen too, that a person can say something themselves. I can often think of a patient who would say "this and that and the other" but would never let *me* say it to them, because if I said it, they would have a realization. So I don't want to say that realizations only occur if the analyst just sits back—it's what I call a complicated case of observing *how* the person defends themselves against realization and acts of understanding, but that certainly to me is central and it's very closely related to conscience. If you think of conscience as an invitation.

Floor: I wonder if we could continue with the discussion instead of having food and drinks.

I feel we shouldn't do that. I know the organizers have put on a farewell reception and when I was at the Tavistock working here, there were a great number of formal meetings, and I came to the conclusion that some of them were to prevent real meetings, and I think sometimes in a reception you can have a real meeting.

Closing remarks

Isca Wittenberg

Somebody said yesterday already to me, "I am dreading tomorrow and the ending", and it is quite obvious that we don't want to end. There is so much to discuss, so much to think about. But the reality is always the time. I'm enormously happy that we have had this conference. It's always been my great desire to bring, to make bridges between different schools of thought, between different religions, between different outlooks, and to bring the Tavistock and spirituality together is really quite wonderful for me! I want to say just a word about fraud, because I feel I am in a bit of a fraudulent position, as if I was responsible for this conference. It is true that I initiated it and interested people in the Tavistock in it, but it actually happened when I was in Karnac and speaking to Mr Sacerdoti, and we talked about Neville's forthcoming book, and we both thought how nice it would be if Neville could have a prolonged meeting on the subject that so concerns us and him, rather than just a lecture, which he had done in the Institute of Psychoanalysis twice before, and so this is how it came about. But really the person who has carried all the burden and the difficulties of the organization—and there have been plenty—is

Jonathan Bradley, so I want to make quite clear, I want to get out of this fraudulent position! What Jonathan Bradley said to me, having met Neville, was "What a brave man!", and he kept on saying "Isn't he brave?" Well, I think he is enormously brave to question dearly held views of analysis and schools of thought, to question some of the aspects of religion really does take bravery, to take these very important hot subjects on board. I think we have seen a demonstration of Neville's bravery throughout these meetings, and I think he has invited us to be equally brave, to strip some of the trappings or some of the distortions or some of the non-essential, non-spiritual aspects out and think about them, to refine our language and to really think what is essential, what is necessary, what is true, and for that I think we are all very grateful, and we have a lot of work to do.

Jonathan Bradley: Well, thank you very much, Isca. I'd just like to really use a few minutes to extend my thanks to different people. Clearly, as Isca said, this was a new idea, and it seemed to me that actually somebody who gave it his support from the beginning was Anton Obholzer, the chief executive, determined, also with an eye to making a little bit of money, but more determined really that it should also happen within an institution like this. It seems to me that Isca has typically played down her own contribution to that process, but I would also like to thank Jenni Hudson. The problem you have when you want to go in a different area is that you usually don't have databases to allow you to do it, and it really has been quite an interesting exercise in discovering that you have lists which don't fit a particular topic—in fact, something like seven thousand separate invitations for this conference were sent out, including the whole of the UK CP register, and it has been interesting, really broadening our list of contacts. I'd also like to thank Paul Inn, who has made a recording throughout and has been here well outside the hours of the conference, and I hope we will benefit from that having taken place.

Now I just want to finish by trying to say something about how to congratulate us as a whole, because I think we need to be congratulated somehow. I've been struggling with various

CLOSING REMARKS   151

images of how to do this. The clear object that has been a source of irritation but also creation has been this roving mike. I want, just before I say something else, to thank the people who have been mainly responsible for that: that's Christine Alhadef, Sarah Dobson, Rebecca Bergese, and Priscilla Green. I have been looking for images to think about that experience. I don't know if you have read the book and seen the film of William Golding's *Lord of the Flies*. Soon after that begins, two of the survivors, Ralph and Piggy, wander along the beach, and piggy has this great idea: he sees this shell, a conch. He thinks that this could be a really good way of regulating discussion, and so what happens is that whenever anyone wants to speak, this conch is solemnly handed round, and if people try to speak without the conch, he would say, "Wait for the conch! You haven't got the conch!" Now if you haven't seen that, or read the book I think it is worth doing, because it fell short of an image because you know what happened to Piggy in the *Lord of the Flies* when he reminded people he had the conch at an unfortunate time and got a boulder on his head—so there must be a different way really of being able to thank us. I found what is referred to as the shortest parable in Mark's Gospel. It's pithy—New Wine New Skins. Now, I think it's a wonderful image, because the fermentation process made use of the flexibility of an animal skin, which was flexible while the fermentation was taking place and by the time the process was over—though I don't know how they managed to do that—it also became a pretty reliable container, more rigid, but a fermentation process had taken place. Disaster, obviously, if you find a rigid skin and pour wine that's just dying to be fermented inside it, and it seems to me that it is an image that can link usefully, say, to the idea of container–contained, because it does imply that there is a need for some flexibility, certainly, in the container, but there is also a lot of pressure from inside. It seems to me that the kind of questions that have come up in this conference implied, I think, as well as stated: can there be a merging of these two ways of seeing? Shall we shuffle together rather than try to resolve some of the issues? Is there more in here than the container my particular vessel will contain? I think that this *has* been explored, and it seems to me there is room for doing so in the future.

Now I just briefly want to say thank you—a personal thank you—to our speaker. Bertrand Russell drew our attention to the distinction between knowledge by definition and knowledge by experience. Knowledge by experience goes in a very different way and it involves a journey by the person finding out the knowledge. It seems to me we have had a most thorough example of somebody really of someone who has learnt to do that. Thank you very much.

Neville Symington: I think I've been anointed to give the last word! I'd just like to thank Jonathan very much for all the organization, and Jenni Hudson, and I would also like to thank very much Isca Wittenberg and Cesare Sacerdoti, whose conversation I think certainly was the originating type of impulse that gave birth to this child. I'd also like to thank my wife, Joan, who did all the visual aids, but I'd like to thank the participants, all of you, really, because as you realize, this is a journey, and I'm still learning—very much so—and I very much welcome the opportunity to be able to put some of these ideas across and to get feedback, and this is a sort of *alma mater* of mine, and so it has been a great pleasure to come, and I think it has been a very good way in which I have felt the audience has been a participatory audience, and I've learnt certain things. When I said at the beginning, "As long as one gets *one* act of understanding I feel that it's been fruitful": well, I have certainly had at least one that I didn't have before—actually, more than one—so many thanks.

APPENDIX A

The true god and the false god

A patient was late one day because snow on the road had delayed her, and she was angry. I mentioned this to Wilfred Bion in supervision, and he said to me: "You must say to her that god has sent down that snow to get between you and her." There is a god that gets in the way of two people coming to know each other. There is a god who interferes with my thinking; there is a god who demands that I follow his instructions; there is a god who punishes me if I think for myself; there is a god who sanctions my sadism, a god who encourages my masochism, a god who fosters my greed, who fosters my envy, who fosters my jealousy, a god who possesses me but despises me, a god who solves problems by obliterating them.

You may recognize, in this portrait of god, traits with which you are familiar from the reading of the Bible, the Torah, or the Koran. Embodied in these ancient texts are aspects of this god that I have been trying to describe. There are also other aspects, to which I shall come later. This cultural expression is manifest in the psychology of the individual. I can find in myself and in my patients traces of this god. This god is a narcissistic object seen from one particular angle. The narcissistic object is many-faceted, and it is a part of the self that has been expelled and embodied in a figure, or figures, outside. The outer figure is then enveloped by this part of the self, in the way that Wilfred Bion describes:

> The object, angered at being engulfed, swells up, so to speak, and suffuses and controls the piece of personality that engulfs it. [Bion, 1967/93, p. 40]

These are the facets of the narcissistic object. The figure, who is an embodiment of the narcissistic object, is extremely sensitive to any hurt. This is the core of the narcissistic object and is not immediately obvious to external perception. For instance, a patient who installs the analyst as narcissistic object perceives him as a god, as an elevated human being in his/her conscious conceptualization, but unconsciously registers the inner sensitivity to hurt. Patients who are narcissistic are extremely sensitive to hurt, and because they believe that others are the same as themselves, they believe that the analyst is as vulnerable to hurt as they are themselves. In this they may be right or may not be right, but it is a belief that they have that is not put to experimental test.

This narcissistic object gets established in this way. The first thing we infer is that this god is present in the personality as a potential for embodiment. This god never exists as a spiritual reality, but always as a god incarnate in a particular person or institution. The prophets whose sayings are recorded in the Old Testament continually chided Israel for chasing after false gods:

> Trouble is coming to the man who says to the piece of
>   wood, "Wake up!"
>   to the dumb stone: "On your feet!"
> (And that is the oracle.)
> Plated it may be with gold and silver,
> but not a breath of life inside it.
> What is the use of a carved image,
> or for its maker to carve it at all?
> It is a thing of metal, a lying oracle,
> What is the use of its maker trusting this
> and fashioning dumb idols.
>
>   [Habakuk 2:19–20 (*Jerusalem Bible*)]

False gods were gods embodied in statues, trees, rocks, rivers—a type of religious ritual known as *animism*. The prophets attacked this form of worship unmercifully. The ferocity of their attack might give a psychoanalyst a hint that they themselves were subject inwardly to such a worship. It is clear that the prophets were trying to purify themselves and Israel of an embodied god and to substitute for this a pure spiritual reality. However, they never managed to cleanse Yahweh of all anthropomorphic elements. He always remained a possession of the Israelites. It was a god who had chosen this race rather than any others as his favourite son:

> Is Ephraim my dear son?
> Is he my darling child?
> For as often as I speak against him,

> I do remember him still.
> Therefore my heart yearns for him;
> I will surely have mercy on him,
> says the Lord.
>
> [Jeremiah 31:20 (*Revised Standard Version*)]

So the god, as part of the narcissistic structure, is ready for embodiment. But how does the embodiment take place? The answer is that the figure or institution has to be a willing host for such an embodiment. The host then has to demonstrate one of the elements of the narcissistic structure.

I am now going to sketch just one correlate of the god. God and this correlate are just two elements of the narcissistic structure, though under the *Principle of Inclusion* they are one reality with two manifestations. (The *Principle of Inclusion* states that two psychic elements are one and the same but with two manifestations, or it can be conceptualized that one is contained in the other.)

So this correlate of god is a figure who is hurt by the slightest criticism or neglect. In religious devotion this is seen most clearly in the Christian rite known as the Stations of the Cross, where the devotee believes that Jesus, who is God, is deeply wounded by every sin. This rests on a theory of Redemption whereby the sin of Adam was an infinite offence to the Lord Almighty, who then sent His Son to make reparation to God, His Father, for this infinite offence. We see here a god who is deeply wounded by an insult. This devotional attitude gained great strength in the Middle Ages and still continues today in many Christian communities, particularly within the Catholic Church. The Old Testament is also redolent with the theme of Yahweh who has been offended by Israel's infidelities.

It is not difficult to see how this devotional attitude came about. It is the reification of a fundamental narcissistic attitude. It is typified when I am deeply wounded by the smallest slight and nurse this injury down the years. A man met a friend who said to him: "Good Lord, John, you are looking well today. When I saw you last week, I thought you were a bit off-colour...." John was deeply offended that his friend should have said he was off-colour. "Me ... off colour"—what an insult. He was so insulted by it that it entirely wiped out the encouraging statement that he was looking well on this particular day.

I remember an occasion when a friend of mine asked a Spaniard to carry a letter for him to a friend in Spain, whither the Spaniard was going. It used to be a gentlemanly custom in Spain that if you asked someone to deliver a letter by hand, it was bad manners to seal the envelope. My English friend, not well up in this piece of Iberian etiquette, did not know this. The Spaniard was deeply insulted and would never speak with my English friend again.

The other aspect, already adumbrated, is that the wound is tended and nursed as though it were the greatest treasure. Adam's sin was quite a long time ago now . . . but I still hear people beating their breasts about it.

Analyst A said to Analyst B: "Oh, you were analysed by Hans Sachs, were you . . .", and then, looking down his nose, said: "You know, I was analysed by Freud." Analyst B was still offended thirty years later and took revenge on Analyst A quite regularly year after year. The hurt only makes sense if you put in the idea of a godlike ego: "Do you not realize that you are insulting a royal personage? Did you not know that you are insulting the Lord Himself?"

So the extreme sensitivity to self-hurt and godhead are included in one another.

I want now to look at another aspect of this god. Knowledge of this god is not arrived at through thought and reflection. This god is revealed in a moment of ecstasy. The clearest example of this is the way in which Allah was revealed to Mohammed. In the midst of an ecstatic trance the teachings of Allah were revealed to Mohammed, who dictated them and had them transcribed onto tablets, which became the Koran. Muhammad himself was a slave in submission to the Voice of Allah. Thinking, which is an inner creative process, was crushed under the force of the ecstatic experience. In Judaism one needs only to consider these two passages—the first from the Book of Exodus, the second from Isaiah:

> Now at daybreak on the third day there were peals of thunder on the mountain and lightning flashes, a dense cloud, and a loud trumpet blast, and inside the camp all the people trembled. Then Moses led the people out of the camp to meet God; and they stood at the bottom of the mountain. The mountain of Sinai was entirely wrapped in smoke, because Yahweh had descended on it in the form of fire. Like smoke from a furnace the smoke went up, and the whole mountain shook violently.

Louder and louder grew the sound of the trumpet. Moses spoke, and God answered him with peals of thunder. [Exodus 19:16–19 (*Jerusalem Bible*)]

I saw the Lord Yahweh seated on a high throne; his train filled the sanctuary, above him stood seraphs, each one with six wings: two to cover its face, two to cover its feet and two for flying.
And they cried out one to another in this way, "Holy, holy, holy is Yahweh Sabaoth. His glory fills the whole earth."
The foundations of the threshold shook with the voice of the one who cried out, and the Temple was filled with smoke. I said: "What a wretched state I am in! I am lost for I am a man of unclean lips and I live among a people of unclean lips, and my eyes have looked at the King, Yahweh Sabaoth." [Isaiah 6:1–5 (*Jerusalem Bible*)]

Then, within Christianity, one need think just of the Pentecost experience as it is described in the Acts of the Apostles and, also in the same book, the incident that has become known as the Conversion of St. Paul on the road to Damascus, where he was struck down onto the ground and a voice spoke to him from the heavens and he was struck blind.

An authority on Islam has this to say about Muhammad:

From the books of tradition we learn that the prophet was subject to ecstatic seizures. He is reported to have said that when inspiration came to him he felt as it were the painful sounding of a bell. Even in cold weather his forehead was bathed in sweat. [Guillaume, 1976, p. 56]

These are all shamanistic experiences, where a transcendent power is believed to have taken possession of the believer, and in whose power the priest, prophet, or shaman becomes the automatic translator of the godly message. Yahweh tells Jeremiah:

"There! I am putting my words into your mouth" [Jeremiah, 1:9 (*Jerusalem Bible*)]

And the Koran is a record of what Muhammad said while in ecstatic states.

How is a psychoanalyst to understand this phenomenon? I think what I have been describing would be formulated by a psychoanalyst as a split-off part of the self taking possession of the whole personality. I think it occurs because in the narcissistic part of the personality a wound has been incurred, and the god arises, having sustained an infinite insult, and takes over the personality. The rest of the personality is utterly crushed by the overpowering god. An example comes to mind from an incident that a colleague described:

> The analyst had a moment of deep empathic understanding of this woman's deprived childhood. She conveyed this to the patient, and there were a few moments of emotional "togetherness" of a deep kind. Then the cruel event occurred: the session, like an insensate executioner, came to an abrupt end. The woman was hurt to the quick. The next day she would not come into the consulting-room; she declared with emphatic certainty that there were hidden microphones in the room, and no rational argument could dissuade her from her conviction. An irrational god had taken over.

What can be observed as happening in an individual is writ large in the religions of revelation, most particularly Judaism, Christianity, and Islam. I want to make it clear that this god exists in all of us who have a narcissistic structure within us. It is not confined to religious people. I have encountered many patients who are atheists in conscious belief but who are enslaved to an ecstatic god within. Secularization has only changed the external forms, not the inner structure.

The god I have been trying to describe I call a false god in that it deceives the believer into trusting his dictates. He believes passionately in what the god directs. As I have tried to illustrate, this passionate belief cannot be shaken by reason, but it is more than that—the presence of this god precludes the possibility of thought. It is intrinsically antagonistic to thought. The inner correlate of the god is a psyche that is gelatinous in nature, with no source of action within and therefore submissive to the god. There is no option other than to capitulate in total submission. The god and gelatinous substance are two parts of an interlocking system. So the action and speech of a person dominated by such a system is false in another sense: that what is said does not represent the thought of a person. It is a pretend person, something standing for a person that could be there but is not. So this is the false god that exists in individuals governed by narcissism; it is also the god that rules all religious observances of a primitive or superstitious kind. As this is death to all thinking, it is completely right that the scientific community has, for the most part, embraced atheism.

I want now to turn to the true god. This is a god who is grasped through a supreme effort of thought—a god who is a triumph of the thinking process. Traces of this god can be found in Judaism, in Christianity, and in Islam, but it is largely overshadowed by the false god. The true god is reached through a deep and sustained reflection on the nature of reality. In our Western tradition, I think the philosopher who best represents this endeavour has been Spinoza. In the East, the seers who are responsible for the school of thinking that produced the Upanishads showed the first and deepest understanding of what I refer to as the true god. "God" is not a term that is ever used by these seers. They use the following terms: "the THAT", "the Absolute", or just "Reality". Wilfred Bion called this same Reality "O". Through contemplative thought these seers came to understand the absolute character of reality. They also understood that reality is contingent. How these two can coexist is baffling to the mind because they are mutually contradictory. Parmenides ran into this problem when he said that all change is illusion. If reality is absolute, then how can there be change? Parmenides, determined that the human mind should not be declared inadequate to any reasoning task, said that because reality is absolute and because change is incompatible with absoluteness, then change must be an illusion. Yet common sense declares that change does occur in our world. Aristotle believed that he had solved this problem by saying that Reality existed in two modes: Pure Act and Potency. By Pure Act, Aristotle meant what the Seers of the Upanishads meant by the THAT or the Absolute. Potency meant being capable of coming to Absoluteness. However, although Aristotle believed that he had solved this problem, yet he had not. He had given an account of the two horns of the dilemma and refused to deny either aspect, but he had not solved the problem.

We are confronted with this problem: that our minds are not capable of grasping this conceptually. Kant emphasized the limitation of our minds. We do not have the categories necessary to be able to grasp the problem. The progress of evolution may enable our progeny millions years hence to be able to solve this problem. What we need to acknowledge is that the human mind meets here a limitation rather than trying to deny either the Absoluteness or the contingency or changeability of Reality.

This Absoluteness is arrived at through rational reflection and, I believe, probably requires mental discipline and virtue to achieve it. It is entirely different from the revelation of the Judeo–Christian–Islamic god, which is through an ecstatic experience directly or by faith and tradition indirectly. The Absoluteness of Being is grasped through a personal act of insight. Although concentrated mental attention is necessary to achieve it, yet there is no experience here of a being outside myself calling me to obedience, submission, or discipleship. It is my own being understood as Absolute. The latter is the true god: the former is the false god.

Now, you may ask, does this have any relevance to clinical work? I believe it does. I approach it in this way. The seers of the Upanishads realized the Absoluteness of Being *and* that they were part of it. The realization that they were part of it, or rather they were IT, turned it from being a philosophical truth into a religious one. In other words, it rendered a piece of knowledge about their own selves, and this piece of knowledge had a consequence. As Tolstoy said, religion is concerned with the meaning of life and how we should live. Realization about the Absoluteness of the self necessarily has a consequence. I say "necessarily" because the necessary is the essential attribute of the Absolute. This realization led the Buddha, who traced the emotional consequences of this realization, to stress that attachment to what is contingent, to what is passing, is to ignore the central character of our being. It is worth noting, however, that the Buddha also recognized that to ignore or despise the contingent nature of our being was to enact in the religious–moral domain what Parmenides conceptualized philosophically. The famous "middle way" of the Buddha is notoriously difficult to achieve. It requires us to realize the limitations of our minds at the same time as to think continually.

So the Absoluteness of Being is a truth arrived at through reflection. It is the product of thought. The thinking process has produced an intuition that penetrates through into the nature of Being. It is an insight that is grounded in rational processes. I call the Absolute the true god: I call the god revealed in the religions of Judaism, Christianity, and Islam a false god or, rather, a god who is a mixture of the true and the false. Within this religious tradition it has been the role of mystics to purify the revealed god of its anthropomorphic accretions. Due to the fact that they bear a loyalty to their religious cult, they only achieve it on the basis of a split.

* * *

The false god is part of the narcissistic system. Other elements in that system are a denigrated object, a state of being merged with the embodied god, a paranoia towards the embodied god, the psyche in a jelly-like state, and absence of creative capacity. As Bion says in his paper "On Arrogance" (1957), this set-up is the living relic of a primitive catastrophe. It is a traumatic event fossilized.

I have referred to the effect of this godly activity within the personality at the beginning. The concept of *embodiment* is central to understanding the effects. There is no thinking process within the personality but only the appearance of such. *Embodiment* of the thoughts of a god has been substituted for thinking. (Some of these gods have names within the psychoanalytical religion: Freud, Jung, Klein, Bion, Winnicott, Kohut, Balint, and so on—some of you may have heard of them; you can see their statues in those temples belonging to what are known as Psychoanalytic Institutes). The god is embodied within, and his or her thoughts are incorporated in the act of *embodiment*. The embodied god is frequently a person, though it can also be an institution. Due to *coalescence*, person and institution are also frequently fused. The individual in whom this narcissistic structure is operating is then in submissive identification with the god. Through this identification the thoughts and thinking processes of the god are understood, and yet there is always distortion. (Wilfred Bion was once at a Group Relations conference, and he kept hearing speakers saying: "Bion said . . ." or, "Bion did not think . . ." etc. He turned to a colleague and said: "This chap Bion sounds as though he was an interesting person.")

However, the most important aspect is that the creative capacity in the individual is crushed through this embodiment. We are familiar in the psychoanalytic world with the discipleship of one analyst towards another—for instance, Jung towards Freud, Paula Heimann towards Melanie Klein. There is a period of intense submission and then a rebellion. The latter occurs at the moment when the individual is trying to break free from the narcissistic bondage. The rage towards the erstwhile mentor is the projected hatred of the submissive act. It is the submissive act that is hated, but it becomes projected and hypostasized in the outer object. It means that the attempt to achieve freedom has failed. The attempted liberation became perverted. True liberation requires realization that the enslaving principle is the inner submissive act, and total liberation requires an understanding that the enslaving principle is one element in the narcissistic structure.

* * *

The realization of the true god in the personality is the product of an inner creative act. This is in dire contrast to the presence of the false god, which is through an act of submission in which the individual psyche is crushed. The realization of the true god lays a foundation in the personality of respect for the Self. I have spelt "Self" here with a capital letter because it is the THAT. I am IT. I am this necessarily so, not through an act of submission. There is no merger here. THAThood is my nature, it is my being—the THAT demands respect. The THAT in me is the THAT in you and demands respect. An act that conforms to that respect has of necessity to be beneficial to me and to you. It cannot be otherwise.

I want to look at just two aspects of the true god: conscience and symbolism. Both of these are extremely relevant to clinical work. Let us take conscience first. Conscience is the subjective evidence of the Absolute aspect of our being. We feel conscience to be us, yet not us. We experience it as inviting us. To follow conscience is a free act, not an obligation. Associated with the false god are words such as "driven", "obligated", or "compelled", whereas conscience is an invitation within the personality, and following conscience is a free act. The ontological truth that the Absolute is in the contingent finds its subjective realization in the free acceptance of the invitations of conscience. As the following of conscience is respecting the Absolute in which I and you share, then, if I follow the promptings of conscience, it has to benefit me and you. Similarly, if you follow the promptings of conscience, it has to benefit you and me. It follows, too, that if I say "No" to the prompting of conscience, I harm you as well as myself. What I have said so far about conscience may be categorized as "religious", but what I turn to now has a directly clinical application.

The truth to which I want to draw your attention is this: that every time a person follows conscience, his or her ego is strengthened. You may demand my evidence for this. My answer is that it is a conviction born of clinical observation. I do not want you to believe this because I have said it. Go and observe and see whether what I assert is verified. Should your observations not confirm this assertion of mine, then I must ask you to describe the psychological processes that lead to strengthening of the ego. I shall, however, stick to my assertion until I have evidence to the contrary. If what I assert is true, then it must be crucial that the clinician should facilitate the following of conscience. From what I have said, it is clear that the clinician cannot *make* the patient follow conscience. Such a statement is a contradiction in terms, because following conscience is a personal free act.

There are two prescriptions for the clinician that seem to follow from what I have said:

The first prescription is that the clinician be encouraged to follow his own conscience. As he is listening to his patient, a realization may come to the mind of the clinician. However, I may find what has come to my mind extremely uncomfortable. The truth that has come to mind may make it clear that I have been going up the wrong path for months, or perhaps years. I may prefer not to communicate what I have understood to the patient. "I won't", I say to myself and have almost decided when conscience pricks me. . . . Alternatively, I may find the truth that has come to mind extremely painful for the patient and wish to protect him from it, and think, "I won't", then conscience pricks me. . . . That we avoid making interpretations because they are disturbing I am certain. However, if we follow the principle that I have adumbrated above—that is, that if I follow conscience, it is mutually beneficial both to me and the patient, then it follows that if the clinician follows his or her conscience, then this strengthens not only his or her ego but also the ego of the patient.

The second prescription is that the clinician avoid smothering conscience. The prime way in which the clinician does this is by acting in the persona of the false god. The false god persuades, the false god demands, the false god says: "Do it my way." The patient invites me to be god; the patient installs me as god; the patient puts enormous pressure on me to be god and to act accordingly. It is my job as clinician to avoid this pressure. The more I am able to avoid being a false god, the less is conscience smothered. The extent to which we fail to do this as therapists can, to some extent, be measured by the degree to which, in the therapeutic world, it is common to find that a therapist follows the doctrinal position of his or her own analyst or follows the school to which his or her own analyst belongs. I believe that it is extremely difficult to avoid smothering conscience. Following the voice of conscience always means experiencing pain and guilt. This has to mean that it is a path fraught with difficulty and one that all humans fight to avoid. However, it is this difficult path that the clinician is being asked to tread, if he is to assist his patient in the job of strengthening his or her ego.

I want now to turn to the relevance of what I have said about the Absolute to symbolism. I will start this topic thus:

> A patient is covertly attacking the analyst, and the analyst points this out. He has made a transference interpretation. The question is "Why?" Is the patient not free verbally to attack the analyst? What is the particular significance that makes the analyst decide to point this out to the patient?

Of one thing I am sure. Very often the implication is: "You have no right to be attacking me." There are two points here. (1) If this is the analyst's viewpoint, then he or she is operating from the narcissistic structure within him or herself. (2) Even if this is not so, from the analyst's point of view, the patient will frequently view it with that viewpoint as his or her basic assumption. It is a narcissistic principle that I believe that the other is motivated by the same principles as myself, and therefore if I—the patient—would feel entitled not to be accused or attacked, then I will also believe that the Other—

the analyst—is also so motivated. The narcissistic reason, then, for pointing out to the patient that he is subtly attacking the analyst is that he should not be doing this. What, then, is the healthy reason for pointing it out?

We can find the answer to this question if we go back to our fundamental premise about the true god: I am IT or THAT thou art. When the patient is subtly attacking me, the analyst, he is subtly attacking himself. In other words, what he is doing to me is a symbol of what he is doing to himself. The purpose, then, of pointing out to him that he is subtly attacking me is to bring him to an understanding that he is attacking himself. The other way of reaching this is to realize that this paranoia directed towards the analyst is a primitive hatred against his own submissive activity; that it is the embodying activity, the making of a false god, that is attacking him himself. Then, as one looks more closely at the self-damaging activity, it is possible to see the subtle ways in which he attacks his own thinking processes. In fact, it is mentality itself that has been severely damaged—to the extent to which the person is deprived of mentality. It has become so confused and embodied that it is difficult to see that there is a mentality there at all.

Symbolism is the name we give to that process whereby we recognize that an activity that is interpersonal, that is outer, represents what is inner. An ontological understanding of the Absolute tells us why this should be so. The true god then becomes not only the rational basis of symbolism, but also its creator. The false god, on the other hand, is the destroyer of symbolism, the destroyer of the inner.

* * *

I want to conclude by making some more general reflections about the significance of what has been said for the claim that there exists absolute truth. I will try to illustrate this by giving you a vignette. Many years ago I found myself in this situation:

> A psychotherapist was presenting his work with a patient to a committee that was trying to assess his work. In discussing his work it was clear that he considered suicide as an evil to be avoided. The chairman of the committee said to him, in a laid-

back tone: "But don't you think this patient was free to commit suicide if he wanted to?"

Under a false-god morality the only answer to this question would be to say that god forbids suicide as he does murder and so on, but for the person who says, "I don't believe in god"—that is, the false god of revelation—then the only arbiter of truth are my subjective feelings. If I want to commit suicide, why shouldn't I? If I want to murder, why shouldn't I? In the latter case you might answer that if I do, I shall go to prison for life. I might answer that I don't care. I can do as I please. My life is my own, it belongs to me. I can contract Aids if I want, if I have Aids I can infect someone else with it. I can do entirely as I please. I can destroy my own mind if I want, it is my business.

This outlook is at present very pervasive in the developed Western world. It is unfortunately the degenerate child of the Judeo–Christian god. It is an outlook shared by most schools of psychotherapy. The chairman of the committee to which I referred was a psychoanalyst of some eminence. Those psychoanalysts and psychotherapists who do not share his outlook are usually not able to ground their position in a convincing set of arguments. There are certain schools of psychotherapy whose very basis lies in a relativism of values such as this committee chairman espoused. In fact, I believe that it is at present only a small minority who challenge it. I think two consequences follow from this: one is that under such a philosophy there can be no healing of a torn mind, because there is no concept of what a torn mind is; the other is that psychotherapy itself exists as part of a narcissistic culture and therefore does not have the tools with which to heal narcissism. Without transforming narcissism, any healing that we produce is false coinage. It is not the genuine article. I believe that we have a personal and cultural task to address.

APPENDIX B

An exegesis of conscience in the works of Freud

The first mention of "conscience" is in Freud's 71st letter to Fliess, written on 15 October 1897 (Freud, 1950 [1897]), where he quotes the celebrated line from Hamlet:

> Thus conscience does make cowards of us all. [Act III, Scene 1]

Freud goes on to ponder why it is that Hamlet does not avenge his father by killing his uncle even though he kills Laertes and his courtiers without scruple. Freud suggests that Hamlet had himself meditated the same deed against his father (out of passion for his mother). And then he says:

> His conscience is his unconscious sense of guilt. [Freud, 1950 (1897), p. 266]

So Freud here equates conscience with guilt for a deed that has been done, but when the guilt is unconscious, the form of it is in actions—that is, the killing of Laertes and his courtiers as displacement from the uncle because of guilt: if he killed the uncle, it would bring him too close to the intent to kill his father, awareness of which would be too shameful.

In the *Studies on Hysteria*, Breuer refers to conscience as something that strikes the person subsequent to the event:

> A very sick woman, suffering from pathological conscientiousness and full of distrust of herself, felt every hysterical phenomenon as something guilty, because, she said, she need not have had it if she had really wanted not to. When a paresis of her legs was wrongly diagnosed as a disease of the spine, she felt it as an immense relief, and when she was told it was "only nervous" and would pass off, that was enough to bring on severe pangs of conscience. [Freud, 1895d (1893–1895), p. 243]

In other words, when the diagnosis suggested that she had some part in it, she was conscience-struck, whereas once it had been pronounced a "disease of the spine", she felt relief. The implication here is that a pronouncement from on high smothers guilt by an omnipotent act of obliteration. Actually it is not obliterated but goes into displaced acts. Both in this case of Breuer's and the previous use of conscience by Freud the sense of it is of condemnation for an act already committed. Conscience is always used in this sense by Freud.

Freud notes in his paper on "Obsessive Actions and Religious Practices" (1907b, p. 119) that qualms of conscience occur when neurotic or religious ceremonials are neglected. It suggests that these religious practices are attempts to ward off punishment. The sense of it is not necessarily that something bad has occurred, and so the qualms of conscience are neurotic. This was written 16 years before the formulation of the structural model, but the sense of conscience is of a declaration on the part of the superego that the ego is bad. As we shall see, Freud later assimilates conscience to one of the functions of the superego where reproaches from the superego are equated with conscience.

In *Totem and Taboo* (1912–13), Freud devotes a couple of pages to the subject of conscience. A taboo is an external prohibition, and Freud refers to a taboo conscience as being the inhibition in us against breaking the taboo. He makes the distinction here (p. 67) between conscience and guilt, with the former operating prior to the act and the latter subsequent to it. This is the only place where Freud assigns to conscience this function of operating prior to the action.

He then notes the connection between conscience and consciousness manifest in their linguistic similarity, and so he defines conscience thus:

> Conscience is the internal perception of the rejection of a particular wish operating in us [Freud, 1912–13, p. 68]

Here Freud sees the operation of conscience as referring to an accomplished act but in particular to the rejection of a wish, so at this stage conscience is the internal perception of this rejection. Thus Freud sees conscience as a faculty operating in three modes:

a. operating prior to the act;

b. observing the act;

c. castigating the ego for the act that has been committed.

However, the first and second functions of conscience appear only here and in *The Question of Lay Analysis* (1926e). To say this in Freud's own language: throughout the works of Freud, conscience is seen as something ego-dystonic and harmful to the ego. The only instance where conscience appears as ego-syntonic is in *The Question of Lay Analysis*. Even here, where conscience is defined as the observer, it is not difficult to see how this slides easily into that part of the personality that observes the ego and is soon castigating it. Freud goes on to say that there is no reason for the condemnations of conscience. It is just certain and obvious, and he implies that the condemnation is not open to rational enquiry. It has therefore to be ego-dystonic. What comes from conscience is like a dictate from god who cannot be questioned. Freud probably believes that conscience arose from the opposition between two different feelings, one unconscious and the other conscious, where the latter dominates the former:

> ... kept under repression by the compulsive domination of the other ... [Freud, 1926e]

In other words, he here equates conscience with a force that is compulsively dominating, and it is for him the installation within of a taboo. This becomes his established formulation: that conscience is the internalization of an external authority. Freud also defines anxiety as a dread of conscience:

> We cannot help being struck by the fact that a sense of guilt has about it much of the nature of anxiety: we could describe it without any misgivings as a "dread of conscience". [Freud, 1926e, p. 69]

At this stage Freud thinks that anxiety occurs when wishful impulses are repressed. He later came to think that anxiety is the repressing agency itself. He says that the act of repudiation to which he refers in his definition of conscience is unknown, and so the reason for this repudiation is unknown.

In his paper "On Narcissism: An Introduction" (1914c), Freud sees the ego-ideal as a narcissistic construct, and conscience becomes the agency that watches to see when the ego fails to measure up to the goals set by the ego-ideal. Therefore conscience becomes part of the narcissistic set-up. What he describes here is a very familiar picture of the narcissistic structure where the personality is split into an idealized self and a degraded self, with conscience aligned with the idealized part in the role of watcher; but now it is clear—which it was not in *Totem and Taboo* (1912–13)—that this watching is for the purpose of condemnation. In a schizophrenic illness or in paranoid delusions this demonic watcher is projected into outer figures, which may be phantasy ones or real ones (p. 95). In this paper Freud gives another definition of conscience:

> The institution of conscience was at bottom an embodiment, first of parental criticism, and subsequently of that of society [Freud, 1912–13, p. 96]

So it is the idea that that part of the self called the ego-ideal or idealized self looks down upon the part that cannot measure up to its superiority and makes a judgement of contempt and that it is this judging agency that is called criticism. He has changed his definition, so that now conscience is clearly the internalization of an outer critical authority. It has now become an exact equivalent of what he came seven years later to name the "superego". In this paper he also equates conscience with the dream censor (p. 97)—that is, that which prevents taboo wishes from emerging directly into consciousness.

The equation between conscience and what was to become the superego is even clearer in the following quotation from "Mourning and Melancholia":

> Our suspicion that the critical agency which is here split off from the ego might also show its independence in other circumstances will be confirmed by every further observation. We shall really find grounds for distinguishing this agency from the rest of the ego. What we are here being acquainted with is the agency commonly called "conscience". [Freud, 1917e (1915), p. 247]

It is not difficult to see from this that Freud was moving towards his formulation of the superego and his equation of this with conscience. That he saw conscience as a proactive force preventing life-enhancing movements of the emotions is clear in his paper, "A Case of Paranoia . . ." (1915f), where he tells of how a girl's mother to whom she was jealously attached played the part of "conscience" as soon as she made a move towards a member of the opposite sex. It is clear that conscience is an anti-developmental force. Its role here is not to condemn but to prevent movements of emotional development. It is clearly ego-dystonic in the extreme.

In "Our Attitude towards Death", Freud equates conscience with a prohibition:

> The first and most important prohibition made by the awakening conscience was "Thou shalt not kill". [Freud, 1915b, ch. 2, p. 295]

In "Those Wrecked by Success", Freud says that the success of people who achieve in external reality what they had imagined in internal reality provokes an outbreak of disease, and this is due to the

> forces of conscience which forbid the subject to gain the long-hoped-for advantage from the fortunate change in reality. [Freud, 1916d, ch. 2, p. 318]

Again here conscience is seen as a punishing tyrant within the personality.

Later in the same paper he discusses the case of Rebecca, the character in Ibsen's play *Rosmersholm*, who causes Rosmer's wife Beata to commit suicide so she can marry Rosmer. However, when Rosmer proposes to her, she refuses and gives the reason:

> "This is the terrible part of it: that now when all life's happiness is within my grasp—my heart has changed and my own past cuts me off from it." [Freud, 1916d, ch. 2]

Freud comments:

> That is to say, she has in the meantime become a different being; her conscience has awakened, she has acquired a sense of guilt which debars her from enjoyment. [Freud, 1916d, ch. 2, p. 325]

It is clear, however, from Freud's commentary on what has awakened conscience that we are talking of a rigid superego-like structure that condemns her. Yet in his whole commentary this is not entirely the position, because it is conscience that awakens her guilt—that is, brings it to awareness.

In the editorial foreword to *Beyond the Pleasure Principle* (1920g, p. 4), Strachey refers to a special self-observing and critical agency in the ego; he refers to it as the ego ideal, the censor, and conscience synonymously.

In *Group Psychology and the Analysis of the Ego*, Freud equates conscience with "social anxiety":

> It has long been our contention that "social anxiety" is the essence of what is called conscience. [Freud, 1921c, pp. 74–75]

It is the notion that it is based on fear of disfavour from those outside—that if it were not for fear of punishment from society, we would commit murder or rape. But for this external restraint, that is what we would do, so conscience becomes fear of the external constraint. It fits with Freud's Oedipal drama, where we fear castration from the father. Father becomes generalized to society and its norms and conscience the voice of father's reproaches. Freud specifically makes this point in *Inhibitions, Symptoms and Anxiety*:

> ... the father has become depersonalized in the shape of the super-ego ... [Freud, 1926d (1925), p. 128]

In *The Ego and the Id* (1923b) Freud says explicitly that the origin of conscience is intimately connected with the Oedipus complex. It is clear—especially in his later works, such as *Civilization and Its Discontents* (1930a) and *The Future of an Illusion* (1927c)—that it is the external threat of punishment that deters members of society from rape, murder, and pillage. Conscience is therefore within the personality the fear of the authority that will punish if any of these misdemeanours are committed. It is worth noting that there is in Freud no place for the possibility of transformation of desire, and therefore the ego-syntonic role of conscience has virtually no place in his system.

Conscience is the repository in the personality for the authority of the group (p. 85). Its power can be put of out action by an intensification of emotion brought about through the pressure of the group. I think he means here a smaller group within the larger society. In this paper Freud defines a couple as a group, and therefore the sexual passion between two people or the hypnotic phenomenon in a couple or small group can temporarily obliterate conscience. Thus Freud says that conscience, as the critical agency, is totally silent when someone is in love because the loved object has been set up in place of the ego-ideal (p. 113), and no criticism can be tolerated about the loved object. In a similar way he says that in the hypnotic trance the moral conscience may show compliance.

In this paper Freud defines conscience as that part of the ego which behaves cruelly to the other part. He later came to name it the superego. So here it is not just an observer but the cruel actor. He says that moral conscience (p. 110) as the repressor is heir to an original narcissism. He is here reiterating what he said in his paper on narcissism—that is, that the ego ideal is part of the narcissistic set-up, and therefore, as conscience is either synonymous with the ego-ideal or one of its functions, it is a consequence of narcissism. Conscience, then, is part of a pathological organization. Freud makes the following very insightful remark about narcissism:

> [it] gradually gathers up from the influences of the environment the demands which that environment makes upon the ego.... [p. 110]

It is therefore because of the narcissistic structure that a person is capable of being exploited by an external person, and it is because of this structure that conscience becomes a castigator. Freud recognizes here that it is the narcissistic structure that scoops the external world into an object of persecution to the ego. In other words, it is not society or culture in itself that is repressive of the instincts, but the repressiveness depends upon whether the outer environment has been internalized according to narcissistic principles or according to healthy ones. It is for this reason, I believe, that Freud reached the climax of psychological understanding in his papers "Mourning and Melancholia" (1917e [1915]), "On Narcissism: An Introduction" (1914c), *Group Psychology and Analysis of the Ego* (1921c), and *The Ego and the Id* (1923b), where he formulated the idea of narcissistic identification and the way this effected internalization of figures in the outer world and of society generally. In his later "sociological papers" he seems to have forgotten this and reverted to the idea that society is repressive in all circumstances; he lost thereby the hold he had on the differential processes of internalization. Had he continued his study of narcissistic identification, he might have examined the question of how conscience differs in narcissistic internalization and in internalization that is normal. The question we should like to ask Freud is: what does the personality structure look like when the narcissistic structure has dissipated? . . . when the individual psyche is largely freed of these processes?

Freud says that a persecuting conscience can be got rid of by projection. Someone, he says in "Some Neurotic Mechanisms in Jealousy, Paranoia and Homosexuality", who projects his jealousy into another becomes acquitted of his conscience and so avoids feeling persecuted from within (1922b, p. 224). Of course, he will feel persecuted by the outside person, but this is less painful. However, Freud does not go into this at this stage because it goes counter to his theory that persecution comes about as the result of the internalization of an external critical authority. It makes one ask whether Freud's theory of the internalization of an external authority is itself a projection. Later, in *Civilization and Its Discontents* (1930a), he says that the severity of the superego is not only because of the severity of the external authority, but because the subject's own desires to attack that authority have been incorporated into the superego; I think this is the only passage where his insight into the influence of narcissistic identification on the outer figure comes into play again. It is an aspect of his view that it is the narcissism that sweeps up the external world that makes the inner world persecuting. However, he does not apply the consequences of this theory of narcissistic identification in his "sociological papers" as a whole; it only appears in one passage in *Civilization and Its Discontents* (1930a), where it is at odds with what he says in the rest of the paper; in *The Future of an Illusion* (1927c) it disappears altogether. There was in Freud the dawning of a different theory that is not consistent with the dominant one in these papers and would have required an overthrow of his more general position. I do not think that it would have been against his nature to overthrow his theory and replace it, as he had overthrown other theories some three times before, but for some reason he did not do this when he came to write the "sociological papers".

In *The Ego and the Id* (1923b), Freud says that the conscience and self-criticism can be unconscious (p. 26). He does not say exactly how this is, but I presume he means that when a person is criticizing from the outside, he does not realize that he is criticizing himself from within:

> The tension between the demands of conscience and the actual performances of the ego is experienced as a sense of guilt. [1923b, p. 37]

The implication is that the ego cannot obey the demands of conscience, and therefore it is a guilt-producing agency. It is a consequence of a broken ego. The idea that the structural model with the severe superego is a consequence of a broken ego is not something that Freud explores directly, but it is implied in some of his statements, such as when he says that the "reproaches of conscience" (p. 53) are typical of obsessional neurotics—therefore clearly implying that this harsh conscience is pathological.

Fear of castration by the father is primary, and fear of conscience and death follow from it. In this formula, however, the fear of castration arises when parental or societal laws have been disobeyed (pp. 57–58). Does Freud mean here that conscience can punish with death? That suicide occurs through guilt is frequently the case, and perhaps he means that guilt is the unconscious determinant in other deaths as well.

In "The Economic Problem of Masochism" Freud says:

> We have attributed the function of conscience to the super-ego. [Freud, 1924c, p. 166]

Then he says, a little further on:

> The ego reacts with feelings of anxiety (conscience anxiety) to the perception that it has not come up to the demands made by its ideal, the super-ego. [Freud, 1924c, p. 167]

Freud attributes guilt—pangs of conscience—to the idea that society has proscribed some behaviour, that this proscription has been internalized in the superego, and that guilt arises if the ego disobeys this command. As we shall see later, this is at variance with the view that conscience may prompt an individual to act contrary to the injunctions of a particular society.

Freud's view rests on the assumption that the individual is made up of untamed impulses and that it is an external authority that imposes restrictions; when this authority is internalized, it becomes responsible for "domesticating" the individual.

Freud was, especially in his later years, struck by the severity of the superego, and he tried to account for it. He suggests that the superego arises through an identification with the parents (1923b, p. 30; 1924c, p. 167). Identification occurs concurrently with a desexualization or sublimation, and it takes place after the erotic component no longer has the power to bind the destructiveness that was combined with it. The destructiveness defuses into the superego and makes it harsh. Hence in "The Economic Problem of Masochism" he says:

> As I have said elsewhere, it is easily conceivable that, thanks to the defusion of instinct which occurs along with this introduction into the ego, the severity was increased. The super-ego—the conscience at work in the ego—may then become harsh, cruel and inexorable against the ego which is in its charge. Kant's Categorical Imperative is thus the direct heir to the Oedipus Complex. [Freud, 1924c, p. 167]

Kant's categorical imperative does not have the support of rational enquiry. It is the voice of the god of Abraham, Isaac, and Jacob, which is an object of belief without rational support. It is this god who, Durkheim thought, was responsible for binding society into a cohesive organization. Freud saw the superego as the habitation of this harsh figure within the structure of the personality. What this god particularly requires is the renunciation of the sexual instinct. This is why Freud thinks that

> Conscience and morality have arisen through the overcoming, the desexualization, of the Oedipus Complex. [Freud, 1924c, p. 169]

It is through this desexualization that the harshness of the superego gains its force (p. 169). Freud came to think that the sadism of the superego is to be explained by the cultural restriction of the aggressive instincts (p. 170). In *Civilization and Its Discontents* (1930a) Freud posits that in any human culture there is a superabundance of aggression, and society copes with this by demanding, as it were, that the individuals in that culture suck in this poison for the sake of the wider group. This sadistic poison is then channelled onto the poor ego of each individual instead of being discharged outwardly in war and savagery.

It is worth noting here that Karl Abraham, one of Freud's most insightful followers, did not think that the individual human being was of necessity at war with society. He believed that the state of antagonism between the individual and society such as Freud described was true only of individuals who were stunted in their emotional development and that the mature individual overcame this dichotomy in himself.

In *The Question of Lay Analysis* Freud uses conscience in a sense that is different from his use of it both before and after this paper. He thinks of it here in its ego-syntonic function:

> If a patient of ours is suffering from a sense of guilt, as though he had committed a serious crime, we do not recommend him to disregard his qualms of conscience and do not emphasize his undoubted innocence; he himself has often tried to do so without success. What we do is to remind him that such a strong and persistent feeling must after all be based on something real, which it may perhaps be possible to discover. [Freud, 1926e, p. 190]

This passage give a contradictory message. Freud seems to be saying that conscience is about something real that needs attention, and then he refers to the person's undoubted innocence. So are the qualms of conscience based on some real act the person has committed and that Freud intends to find out, or is the person innocent? In other words, has the person just internalized a cultural injunction? The other anomaly in this paper is that in all other places Freud refers to conscience as a function of the superego, but in this paper it is the other way around (p. 223): he seems to imply that conscience is the prime faculty. This would allow for the possibility that he thought of the superego as a deformation of conscience. I think this anomaly could only be resolved through textual criticism of the original German—something that I have neither the training nor the knowledge to be able to do.

That conscience is the fear of being found out, either by an outer authority or an inner one, is enunciated most clearly by Freud in *Civilization and Its Discontents* in the following passage:

> This . . . is the reason why it makes little difference whether one has already done the bad thing or only intends to do it. In either case the danger only sets in if and when the authority discovers it. [Freud, 1930a, p. 124]

"Thou shalt not be found out" lies at the heart of this morality. Taken on its own, this is almost a psychopathic position. The following statement a bit further on makes it clear that Freud does not consider that such a position deserves the name of bad conscience:

> This state of mind is called a "bad conscience"; but actually it does not deserve this name, for at this stage the sense of guilt is clearly only a fear of loss of love, "social anxiety". [Freud, 1930a, pp. 124–25]

Conscience is a signal fear of punishment. Then there is a transition, Freud says, whereby the external authority becomes internalized in the superego. He says here that the reason the superego torments the ego is that the latter's role is to pass on the tradition to the next generation. This social necessity is driven by the instinct for survival.

The fact that Freud considers reward in eudaemonic terms is also clear from the following passage:

> . . . it is precisely those people who have carried saintliness furthest who reproach themselves with the worst sinfulness. This means that virtue forfeits some part of its promised reward. [Freud, 1930a, p. 126]

What he says here is only partly true. Saints and holy people do reproach themselves, and some are given to excessive statements about their sinfulness, which would suggest the operation of the superego; but the consciences of people who have dedicated their lives to the pursuit of virtue are more refined, and they also derive peace and contentment from following it. There are many passages from mystical writings that illustrate this.

As has already been said, it is here in *Civilization and Its Discontents* (1930a) that Freud shows that he believes that the severity of the superego is not only because of the external authority but because of the ego's own attacks on that authority (pp. 129–130). Also—unlike in *The Question of Lay Analysis*—he maintains here that conscience is a function of the superego:

> This function consists in keeping watch over the actions and intentions of the ego and judging them, in exercising a censorship. [Freud, 1930a, p. 136]

Freud equates the need for punishment with masochism. The general tenor he adopts is that the operation of conscience and the anxiety it provokes is a pathology to be cleared up. The notion of a healthy conscience seems to be absent—except in *The Question of Lay Analysis* (1926e). Obeying the superego prevents happiness for the ego (1930a, p. 143).

In "Dostoevsky and Parricide" (1928b) Freud says that the normal processes in the formation of conscience must be similar to the abnormal ones. He goes back here to describing the superego/conscience as the internalization of a severe, harsh father, which is what he calls abnormal. He seems to be saying therefore that normal conscience is also pathological in nature (p. 185).

In "Lecture XXXI" of the *New Introductory Lectures* (1933a), Freud says that the persecution of being watched and so on comes from a projection of the critical superego. He says that being observed is a precursor for being punished (p. 59), and he talks of conscience not *allowing* the ego to do something. Conscience *forbids*. It is clear that by this time he has thought out the functions of the superego more clearly. The superego has three functions: self-observation, conscience, and the maintenance of an ideal (pp. 60, 66). Self-observation is a necessary preliminary to a judgement of conscience. Whereas in *Totem and Taboo* (1912–13) Freud defined conscience as this self-observing function, he now sees this as separate and conscience as the critical judge in the personality. In "Lecture XXXII" (1933a) he makes the point that conscience lives in the unconscious. In his paper *Why War?* (1933) he says that conscience is the internalization of the death instinct (p. 211).

In *An Outline of Psycho-Analysis* (1940a [1938]) Freud refers to the judicial function of the superego, which is called conscience (p. 205). In the same paper he refers to the torments caused by the reproaches of conscience that correspond to the child's fear of loss of love. This is the idea that runs through Freud's works: that the fear of loss of love of the parents becomes transferred to conscience. Fear of loss of love from the superego is what causes the torture when a "sinful" act has occurred.

We must conclude that in all Freud's works the assumption is that conscience is bad, a persecutor, and something pathological in the personality. It remains now to see whether this is the accepted meaning of conscience among moral philosophers, scholars in religious studies, and moral theologians and, more generally and most importantly, whether Freud's use of the word is what is understood by the educated public and whether it is this that has been understood by great writers and poets as the meaning of conscience.

*　*　*

What starts as a small investigation frequently turns out to be a matter that requires hours, weeks, and months of scholarly research. What I thought would be an easy matter to dispose of becomes something much more complex, requiring considerable historical enquiry. My brief investigation into this is as follows: that conscience [being the translation of *suneidesis*] appears rarely in classical Greece and was not a common concept in the Greco–Roman world, though, for instance, Socrates says of those who had perjured themselves at his trial: "Let their consciences punish them." The person who launched the concept into the currency of our language was St. Paul. He alone of the New Testament writers pioneered the term. His use of it accords with that of Freud. It is the inner accusation for a deed that has been committed. This is the unequivocal meaning of it throughout St. Paul's writings, and it continued to be the meaning of conscience within Christendom.

In more recent centuries conscience acquired a broader meaning. I cannot say exactly when this occurred, but I surmise that it was with the emergence of the Enlightenment within European thinking. Rousseau certainly emphasized that conscience, not reason, was our guide to action:

> Conscience does not tell us the truth about objects but the rule of our duties; it does not tell us what we must think but what we must do; it does not tell us right reasoning but right action.
> [J. J. Rousseau, *Nouvelle Heloise*, quoted in Hampson, 1971]

With the secularization of social institutions was there to be no foundation for ethical thinking? Conscience, as used by St. Paul and by Freud, remained but two important dimensions accreted to its use.

Conscience came to be used as that faculty in us which invites the individual psyche towards what is right. In other words, conscience came to be used as the faculty that invites the individual towards righteousness and also points to the path where that is to be found. Bertrand Russell puts it thus:

> The orthodox view is that, wherever two courses of action are possible, conscience tells me which is right, and to choose the other is sin. [Russell, 1974, p. 190]

Therefore conscience has acquired the meaning of a guide that points the individual psyche in the direction of righteousness. The word "righteousness" has such appalling connotations for us today because it suggests a right path ordained from above by a superior power, most frequently either god or a god-equivalent. However, the modern sense of it is as the faculty that points to a path that is inwardly right for this individual and indicates the right path for the individual, with the implication that it may require the individual to repudiate the sanctions of external authority. So Hannah Arendt (1964) said of Eichmann that he was not a hater of Jews, but his conscience told him to obey the orders of his Nazi superiors. In other words, a bad conscience is one where the dictates of external authority are internalized. It suggests that a good conscience is something freed of such external injunctions, where it may invite the individual psyche to act in opposition to an outer command.

In his *History of European Morals*, Lecky says:

> Conscience, whether we regard it as an original faculty, or as a product of the association of ideas, exercises two distinct functions. It points out a difference between right and wrong, and when its commands are violated, it inflicts a certain measure of suffering and disturbance. [Lecky, 1913, p. 62]

So, in addition to the function that Freud attributes to conscience, in post-Enlightenment thinking it has acquired two other functions: that of an inner guide to what is right and of a function that is individual and not an internalization of the injunctions of external authority. The post-Enlightenment idea of conscience as a *personal* guide is absent in Freud.

Paradoxically, no one emphasized this personal status of conscience more than did John Henry Newman. I say "paradoxically" because he was leader of the Oxford Movement in the Anglican Church, and then, on conversion to the Roman Catholic Church, he went on to become one of its cardinals. Yet, despite his devotion to the Catholic faith, he said that if he had to choose between obeying the Pope or his conscience, he would always choose to follow his conscience. Like Hannah Arendt, one presumes that automatic obedience to an external authority would be a sign of a bad conscience. Newman describes the faculty of conscience in this way:

> Conscience is a personal guide, and I use it because I must use myself; I am as little able to think by any mind but my own as to breathe with another's lungs. Conscience is nearer to me than any other means of knowledge. [Newman, 1888, pp. 389–390]

The conclusion seems to be that Freud sees conscience as condemnation for a crime committed and as the internalization of external authority. It seems that, according to post-Enlightenment usage, Freud's definition of conscience is too limited. He has reverted to the Pauline use of the word and does not allow for conscience as an inner guide to right action. If conscience functions as the internalization of the dictates of external authority, such as in the extreme case of Eichmann, then this is what has been declared to be "bad conscience". What Freud describes as "conscience" is, then, "bad conscience" or a pathological conscience. The question that then arises is: "Does Freud's psychology incorporate what is called 'good conscience', and if so, under what name does it appear in his works?" . . . or is the concept absent in Freud?

A harsh conscience, the internalization of an external authority, occurs through narcissism. It is a property of the narcissistic set-up that it sweeps the external authority into its internal psychic sphere. What Freud describes is the pathological emotional activity that arises as a consequence of narcissism. A healthy conscience, a sane conscience, escapes his attention.

I want to add a final footnote, which requires more investigation. What I refer to as "good conscience" or the post-Enlightenment meaning of conscience can, I believe, also be understood as a judgement upon an act committed. If this is the case, then what differentiates a conscience that is ego-syntonic from one that is ego-dystonic? I believe it is whether the act committed is believed to be reparable or irreparable. I put this in as a final aside because the question of how these two are to be differentiated will take us upon another trail.

APPENDIX C

Envy: a psychological analysis

Since the advent of *Envy and Gratitude* in 1957, the word "envy" has flooded the clinical literature within psychoanalysis. It has been particularly profuse within the Kleinian School, but this has overflowed into the clinical descriptions both of the Independent School and that of the Classical Freudians. What I attempt here is a psychological analysis of envy, because we assume that we all know what we mean by it. I think the meaning that we attribute to it is something like the following:

Envy is hatred of another for having a treasure I do not possess.[1]

The focus of this definition is upon the other. This, I believe, derives from folk religion and throws no light upon why this entity is damaging to the author of the envy. If a psychoanalyst is asked

"Why should I not envy another?"

I believe the questioner will be answered with a moralistic answer:

"It is harmful to another person to hate him for a treasure that he possesses. Therefore it is bad."

Someone who is satisfied with contract theory might elaborate this further and point out that something that is bad for another is harmful for society and therefore ultimately to the person himself and so should be shunned. However, this is dubious and very far from psychoanalysis, which is concerned with the immediate effects of an individual's emotional activities. Let us therefore try to build up a picture of envy as revealed by psychoanalytical investigation.

Idealization: the first stage of envy

Envy is inseparable from idealization. The treasure in the envied one exists in the bosom of someone who is idealized. [The fact that this person is also denigrated we shall come to later]. I believe that this is a clinical fact: that envy and idealization always co-exist. This leads me to my first supposition:

- Idealization is part of the structure of envy.

Working on the assumption that this is so, it becomes necessary to look at how idealization occurs. What are the psychological activities that account for it? Let us try first to edge towards a definition of "idealization":

- It is a perception of the other in which the goodness is exaggerated and the badness minimized.

It might be more accurate to define it slightly differently:

- It is a perception of the other in which the virtues are exaggerated and the vices minimized.

In both of these definitions, the focus is upon the moral qualities of the individual or group. But idealization is also used of those who have excelled in the practical or literary arts. The definition here then would be:

- It is perception of the other in which excellence is exaggerated and deficits are minimized.

This last definition is probably more satisfactory as it can be applied to the field of ethics, aesthetics, or practical arts.

The point to note is that this defines idealization as a deformation of perception. It would be possible to substitute "judgement" for "perception". I have chosen "perception", however, as it conveys immediacy, whereas judgement suggests a time-delay. However there is always judgement present in perception. One of the faults of faculty psychology is that it creates the false belief that perception, cognition, and motivation are discrete entities. In judgement there is always perception and vice versa. Another way of defining this defective perception is to call it an illusion. From this angle we could define "idealization" thus:

- An illusion in which excellence is exaggerated and deficits minimized.

This has the advantage that it can refer to subject or object.

What I want to address myself to now is not *why* an idealization occurs but *how* is it accomplished. What is the emotional process that fashions this particular illusion? The excellence in the self is projected into the object, and the deficits in the object are ingested into the self. The illusory perception is the result. To speak with psychological accuracy, we need to say that the perception records correctly what has emotionally occurred.

It is clear now why envy is damaging to the personality. The envious person has rid himself of what is of worth in him and ingested what is valueless. This way of acting is according to an acquired pattern but is also maintained through an assembly of minute actions that accumulate and structure the long-term character structure. The analyst's job is to interpret these projections of excellence and ingestions of deficit as they occur in the session. The slow erosion of these activities leads to a destabilization of the long-term character structure. As these interpretations are made, the patient comes into possession of those elements of worth within him and ceases to ingest the deficits of others. If this is done with constancy, the patient's perception changes. This I believe is evidence in favour of my view that perception is the accurate recording of what has emotionally occurred. It is that emotional activity is the governing hand of perception.

Idealization is the first stage of envy but also its foundation. I believe I have clinical evidence that if a patient *realizes* this, then the rest of the structure of envy crumbles. I now want to consider the remaining structure, which I call the second stage of envy.

Damage to the object: second stage of envy

When the individual has accomplished the first stage of envy, he is deprived of self-worth and is full of shit. He resents this state of affairs. He is not aware of these "invisible" emotional activities that have brought it about and so blames outer figures for his plight. The subject is now impoverished and the object is enriched and the object is hated. The principles of the process whereby the idealization has come about also apply here. The subject's own activities are obliterated in his mind, and those of the object become magnified. The magnification results from the projection and ingestion. So, for instance, a man was aware of his father's authoritarian attitude but not of his own emotional indecision which provoked it. It is not that the authoritarian attitude was not there but that it becomes hated through the magnification due to his own emotional activities, which we summarize as "indecision". This attribution of an activity in the subject to a static quality in the object I have called *hypostasization*. The more common way of naming such a procedure in psychoanalytic discourse is to say that the son projects his own authoritarian attitudes into the father. This does not, however, explain how the psychological process works. For instance, the son's emotional indecision is left out of the account. An account that says the son's authoritarian attitudes are projected into the father is a crude account that by-passes the "how" of the process. Also, if it is interpreted in this way by the analyst, it frequently becomes an accusation. An accusation has occurred rather than an interpretative understanding of the process.

So *hypostasization* may be defined thus:

- A process whereby emotional activities of the subject become perceived as static qualities in the object.

Hypostasization, then, is another aspect of the idealization. It is not only that the projection and ingestion occur, but because these activities are unconscious, only their consequence is perceived. Again all this needs to be interpreted so that the patient is able to take possession of his own activities and thereby alter them if he so desires. My experience is that patients often do desire to alter them. I believe that is why they are in the consulting-room.

Once this *hypostasization* has occurred, then the subject, out of resentment, stirs up the object, controls the object, attacks the object, and so on. It is this stage of the envy that Melanie Klein describes when she talks of expelling faeces into the breast, attacking mother's body, her babies, and so on. This is the reason why paranoia is always part of the picture in any accurate phenomenological description of envy. The projection of faeces and urine, to use Melanie Klein's language, occurs because the inner worthlessness is loathed and is projected by the omnipotent figure in the personality. The inner worthlessness arises from the presence within of envy, greed, jealousy, and omnipotence *which is hated*: "I must be utterly contemptible to have all this envy, jealousy and greed inside me", the person says to himself. Paranoia is the hatred for the inner entity now existing outside. It also explains why the paranoid person is tied to his object: he cannot be separated from part of himself

Focus on the subject rather than object

Melanie Klein does speak very clearly about the way envy strangles the creative and generous impulses in the subject. She also gives considerable emphasis to what is done to the object; how mother's body, babies, and breast are attacked. I believe that this focus steals the light away from the activities of the subject and how these are damaging to the subject. It is not that she does not speak about the way the subject's generous impulses are strangled, but that this is overshadowed by her focus on the object.

There is no doubt that to be the object of sustained resentment for months and years tests emotional endurance to the limit. Being the target of such envy makes it extremely difficult to analyse the psychological processes that generate it. Yet it may be that the fact that they are not analysed and psychologically understood is the reason why it endures so relentlessly. Bion said that the psychotic patient stirs up the resistance in the analyst. A re-phrasing of this would be to say that the second stage of envy smothers from view the first stage. My contention is that it is the analysis of the first stage that disintegrates the envious constellation.

* * *

The psychological structure of envy is misperceived if it is viewed in isolation. Melanie Klein associates it with greed and jealousy, both noting the connection and the difference. To these two needs to be added omnipotence. We are talking now of an envy where first and second stage is established and kept in being. This means that the action pattern of both the first stage and the second is in constant operation. The individual is ridding herself of her own worth into the object and introjecting the latter's bad qualities into herself and then, in her bitter resentment, ridding herself of these into the object. However, the third party (father) has to be kept out because he represents the eye of awareness which, when fully functional, prevents the emotional activities peculiar to both the first and second stage of envy. Keeping out father is the role of jealousy.

I use almost carelessly the phrase "keeping out father", but who keeps him out? The all-powerful god referred to as "omnipotence" in analytic literature. In a similar way the emotional activities specific to the first stage of envy are obliterated through this omnipotent agent. God has the power to obliterate. In fact, the reality is obliterated through being split up and expelled, but it is god who does the splitting up and the expelling. When in the first stage of envy worth is evacuated and deficits ingested, it is god who is responsible for preventing awareness and, in the social group for introducing the anodyne word "idealization", to draw a veil over the violent activities under its umbrella. It is a social collusion against awareness.

"Omnipotence" also is a poor word, because although it is a noun, it is not an agent. It is an attribute of god, like "kindness" might be an attribute of John Smith, but kindness is not an agent that acts. One might say that John Smith acts with kindness and therefore it is adjectival grammatically. In a similar way, god acts with omnipotence and his action in the personality is to split, expel, and ingest, which prevents awareness.

Envy is accompanied by greed, jealousy, and omnipotence. The omnipotence is incarnate in a figure, figures, or an institutional group. In the analytic situation its typical form is to be located in the analyst and patient. An interpretation about "envy" is seen, I believe, in two divergent yet united ways. On the one hand, the patient hears the analyst declaring, "This quality in you which I name envy is bad, it should not be in you." This is god making a declaration. For the patient, it is not an interpretation. The other way in which the patient hears this statement is that it is coming from the bleat of an emotionally wounded child—that when the *analyst* points out envy he has done so because he is persecuted by it. It is the definition of a psychological process from the point of view of the attacked and injured object. All the seven deadly sins, of which envy is one, have been defined in this way, and that is why they are words appropriate to a primitive religiosity and quite unsuitable for a psychological discipline.

I want to make sure that I am properly understood here. I am not saying that envy should not be interpreted—quite the opposite. I am saying that its full psychological structure needs to be understood and interpreted firmly and clearly. To do this successfully, each of the elements in the structure needs to be kept in mind. So, for instance, when the analyst feels himself under relentless and resentful attack, it is a mistake to point out envy, using the word. Once the structure is understood, he knows that god in the personality is responsible for it. He knows also that it has been preceded by the activities peculiar to the first stage of envy. He knows also that it is related to jealousy and to greed. He has quite a menu to choose from. His choice will be dictated by what the patient is bringing at any one moment in time.

I believe, speaking very generally, that Kleinian analysts tend to fall into the trap of speaking of the envy in the patient from the seat of god. The analysts of the Independent Group in the British Society are so fearful of being moralistic that they try to soothe the condemning god away. (I am too unfamiliar with the practice of the Classical Freudians in this regard to be able to comment.) In both cases the envy remains untouched.

Now onto greed. Greed determines the intensity of the evacuation and ingestion both in the first and second stage of envy. It is responsible for turning something of worth into a deficit. I think the way the ingestion of a deficit occurs is that what is attempted is the taking in of a good but it is done with such violence that it damages rather than enriches.

* * *

In his paper "On Arrogance" (1957), Bion says:

> that in the personality where life instincts predominate, pride becomes self-respect, where death instincts predominate, pride becomes arrogance. [p. 86]

I want to argue here that this is the wrong level of explanation. I do not want to enter into the debate on the existence or not of the death instinct but, rather, that all the instincts, whatever they be, are operating at the biological level and that psychology emerges in response to them. This constellation—envy, greed, jealousy, and omnipotence—are, I believe, the presence of trauma in the personality. I think the definition of envy in terms of something congenital in the personality or due to the death instinct arises out of the same definitional practice that uses the word "envy" to define a psychological process—in other words, a definition where a biological process in substituted for a psychological one. The factor that determines whether pride becomes self-respect or arrogance is in the absence or presence of omnipotence.[2]

I was struck some years ago when noticing that the people in whom envy, jealousy, greed, and omnipotence were most deeply implanted were those who had suffered catastrophes in infancy or childhood. At first I said to myself that the latter was in some obscure way consequent upon the former, Later, under the influence of Bion's theory of transformations, I came to think that envy, greed, jealousy, and omnipotence *are* the infantile trauma. Once it is realized how damaging these are to the personality, it becomes clear that in them the trauma still lives. It is the physical trauma that has undergone psychological transformation. The damage to the personality is the invariant; the variables are the physical event in history and the constellation of envy, greed, jealousy, and omnipotence. I feel a conviction about this that I cannot give adequate account for. I know for myself that this perspective has given me a sympathy at the level of knowledge, even if this is frequently marred at the affective level. I have, I believe, achieved some clinical success with such patients which has been greater than before I had this perspective. When I use the word "perspective", I mean not only the traumatic quality of this envious constellation, but also the first and second stage of envy and its relations to its partners: greed, jealousy, and omnipotence.

There is another way of looking at this. Trauma is usually conceptualized as something positively damaging done to the infant. For instance, a mother who projects her anxieties into her baby; a baby who suffers the loss of her mother; a child who is sexually abused by her father. However, *the* trauma is an absence of what should be there. What the infant needs most is *emotional giving*, and it is the absence of this, in whatever form, that is the prime trauma. Emotional absence cannot be conceptualized, just as "nothing" cannot be conceived, so elements are dragged into the vacuum to make badness tangible. The elements that do this service are envy, greed and jealousy. Together they fashion the monstrous object that crushed the human subject.

* * *

I think Melanie Klein did a great service to psychoanalysis by signalling the importance of this factor in the personality, but, as in any science, this was just the first rough outline and is defective through its overemphasis upon the effect on the object, the use of a primitive religious term, and a failure to explain adequately the psychological processes that lay behind it. In my terms she described the second stage of envy, but the not the first. It is unfortunate that followers of Melanie Klein have not developed her first gropings more fully. Death has the unfortunate consequence of endowing the works of the deceased with a paralysing *imprimatur*. Had Melanie Klein continued to live and defy death, she would have developed this first sketch into a finished work of art.

Psychoanalysis is more important than any of the figures who have developed the science and the art. It is my hope that everyone here shares this sentiment.

Notes

1. Melanie Klein defines envy thus: *Envy is the angry feeling that another person possesses and enjoys something desirable* (Klein, 1957). I have changed this definition because envy may not exist as a feeling. In fact, when it is unconscious, it does not, and it is envy of this kind with which psychoanalysis is most concerned. Once it does not exist as a feeling, then the qualifying word *angry* does not apply.

2. It actually depends upon whether the omnipotence is integrated in the personality or disowned.

APPENDIX D

"I feel a fraud"

He was a solicitor, head of his firm. He was a competent lawyer. Yet he said: "I feel a fraud."

Why? I will tell you a story about myself.

When I was doing my undergraduate degree in psychology, I concentrated most of my attention on social psychology, personality theory, motivation, cognition, and perception. However, I had to do courses on classical learning theory as well, and what is more I had to do exams in it. I knew that in particular what the examiners wanted was evidence that students were familiar with the experiments that proved that partial reinforcement was a stronger stimulus to learning than constant reinforcement. Those who have studied this type of psychology will know that one experiment proves one thing, but then a team of researchers do another experiment, which proves a different point of view. These papers were nearly always written by at least four authors, and, so it seemed to me, with long hyphenated names. However, I believed that if I learned a good number of these experiments and each with the names of the authors, it would stand me in good stead with the examiners. So . . . forty-eight hours before the dreaded exam, I set about learning the experiments and tagged each one with the names of the correct researchers. In those days I could commit a series of such names and details to memory quite well. So my head was full of rats, pigeons, mazes, dates, and names. I went into the exam, and did my worst. When the examiner read my paper, he saw that this student had a good grasp of classical learning theory with a striking knowledge of the up-to-date experimental literature. However, what he did not know was that a week later all trace of this knowledge had disappeared utterly from that student's mind. Now I felt a fraud. But why? What had I not done? What would I have needed to have done in order not to feel a fraud?

When I said: "I set about learning the experiments", that is a misuse of the word "learning". I ingested a great scroll of information. I did not ask myself questions like "Why did Karl Lashley devise a jumping-stand for his rats rather than use a maze?" "Why did Precht use spiders rather than mammals to distinguish between drives and excitatory levels?" And as I did not ask myself questions, I never had the experience of suddenly grasping something. There was no act of understanding. This is why I felt a fraud. What I had done in that exam was not technically cheating, but psychologically it was. When I understand something, it is a personal creative act. If you hand me a palette of oil colours and then you see me painting an elephant douching itself at a water-hole, you can see clearly that I am creating something. However, if you see me with a camera in my hand in front of an elephant at the water-hole douching itself and I photograph it, something quite different is happening. For the analogy to work, it would be better to imagine a computer-operated camera set up in a hide that clicked every fifteen minutes; at the end of the day, by chance, there are some photographs of an elephant douching itself. When I memorized those psychological experiments, I had photocopied them into my mind. I had not painted a picture. I felt a fraud.

What I want you to do now is to take what I have said not as a template but as a symbol from which a fire-work display of tracers might be gathered. To return to the solicitor. He not only felt a fraud as a lawyer, but in himself. He felt a phoney husband, an artificial father, and a fraudulent worshipper in his parish church. So what one is positing here is that he has memorized not just the data for a psychology exam, but a schema for living. G. K. Chesterton said that home is the place where you can eat breakfast off the carpet if you want to. Chesterton was not someone who had memorized a schema for living. He had done something else, but I believe my solicitor had "memorized" a schema for living: at a very early stage in his life he had ingested a schema that said: "This is the way to be a man. Follow each direction with exactitude . . .", and that is exactly what he had done. He had followed all the prescriptions to the letter, and this is why he felt a fraud.

If the unfurling of his life had come from an act of creation, he would have felt genuine. This was the reason why he complained to me that everything felt amiss. He had not come because he himself wanted to, but because his wife had demanded that he should come. To live with a fake is exasperating. Wilfred Bion describes a case where he was referred an intelligent young man for analysis, but he discovered that everything said about him proved to be illusory. Then Bion says:

> I used to wonder if I had chosen the wrong job; if I might not have been better off as an ordinary doctor. But ordinary doctors have the same kind of patient. Ordinary fathers and mothers have the same kind of children. Ordinary sisters have brothers like that. Ordinary brothers have sisters like his sister. They all come to psycho-analysis in the end. [Bion, 1974, pp. 112–113]

So his wife could not stand it, and she sent him to a psychoanalyst. I could only stand it because I was curious about fakehood and I only had him for fifty minutes a week. His wife had him for a lot longer, and I doubt whether she was curious about why he was a fake. I suspect his ill temper flooded her emotional reservoir and made curiosity a far-off luxury.

The act of creation I am talking about brings about the presence of a person. Just as the new-born infant has to take a first breath into its lungs to stay alive, so the baby has to generate an act of creation to turn an anatomical mechanism into a person.

Now here's the question that you will all be asking: What is it that enables the infant to generate an act of creation? What is it that prevents it? Let us say with no ambiguity that we do not know. Anything I say now is a guess; anything anyone says is a guess. The only psychoanalyst present in the first year of life is the mother, who is often too preoccupied to function in that way, or if she does, then she does it and is not here giving us a lecture on it. Infant research is a mixture of observation and guesswork. The direction of the guesswork is frequently determined by the individual's own experiential theory. Margaret Mahler believed that only when the infant separated from a symbiotic phase with the mother did it emerge as its own individual person. She said this in Vienna; when she was in the bosom of the psychoanalytic society there, she did not produce her own original work, but only when she separated and crossed the ocean to America did her own creative self come to birth. Her infant research is infused with this experience and also structured her team's observations. What I am going to say is also structured by my own experiential theory.

What I am positing is that what generates the "individual psychological birth" is a creative act. This is what brings the person into being. It implies that if this does not occur, then a person does not come into being. Wilfred Bion's writings are sprinkled with references to the difference between being a person and being just like a person. Winnicott spoke of the false self, which he contrasted with the true self. It means that both distinguished between individuals who are real people and those who are façades, and it was this differentiating criterion that separated the mentally ill from the mentally healthy. For both these clinicians, the suppression of the individual in favour of accommodation to social expectation is the primordial sin. I would like to emphasize that the group out of which the expectation proceeds is invested with godhood. The pathological spectrum originates from this "original sin". Mental health and creativity are rooted in the establishment of a true self as foundation-stone in the personality. Now both Bion and Winnicott thought similarly about this but differed in their guesswork as to how this had come about. My own is closer to that of Bion, but Winnicott's understanding is also present when I consider the effect of trauma on the infant's capacities.

So the way I look at it is this: that it is a creative act that brings the person into being. What existed before was a number of bits or fragments, and the creative act welds them together into a person. The result is not what a chemist would call a mixture but a compound. Bion's clinical technique aimed to assist in bringing this about. As these different parts of the personality surfaced, so he named them, making it possible thereby for that generative creative act to occur which would weld them into that compound that we call a person. Bion pays much attention to those forces in the personality that subvert the possibility of this happening. No analyst, no other person can do it for the individual. Persuasion, or even encouragement, prevents this act from occurring. In clinical practice it is of extreme importance therefore that the analyst neither condemns nor encourages—that she be neither a savage god nor a benevolent one. That emotional act whereby these discrete fragments become welded into one whole emerges from the inner freedom of the individual. If one part is condemned and another validated, the individual will not have available all the parts out of which to generate the person. The *narcissistic constellation* about which I have spoken is an anti-personal system present in the organism.

This is such an important matter clinically that I am going to divert for a moment in order to highlight it. If one of the fragments that the analyst is naming is called envy, or greed, or jealousy, the patient is very likely to hear the analyst implying that this is bad, this is something that should not be there, this is something that is self-destructive. Then, instead of those fragments being available for transformation in the generative act, they become enemies to myself. Then I am in a very bad way. I have only part of myself available, and the other part is not only not available but has become a fifth columnist that attacks the healthy part.

I said to a patient that it seemed to be her greed that made it impossible ever to leave anything aside. She replied:

> "I know it looks like greed from the outside, but from inside it is different. I am desperately looking for something. I do not know what that something is, but I am afraid of missing something in case I lose that which I am trying to find."

I believe that this formulation of hers was accurate. Her search was too "driven", but I am sure the aim was just as she said. The paradox is that an element disowned becomes destructive of the personality, whereas if owned and welcomed, it becomes a source of strength. The person who has expressed this best is Moses de León, the probable author of the Zohar. I quote just this sentence from Gershom Scholem's well-known book:

> ... moral evil, according to the Zohar, is always either something which becomes separated and isolated, or something which enters into a relation for which it is not made. [Scholem, 1995, p. 236]

So the prime focus of our clinical work needs to attend to this tendency to disown and condemn. When I hate an element in myself, I cannot integrate it into my personhood.

The clinical problem I am going to leave you with is this: How do I speak to a patient about envy, about greed, about jealousy without installing myself as a god who condemns? I do not mean that it is not to be talked about, not that it is to be watered down. In fact, I would want to speak about these in such a way that their damaging effects are seen only too clearly—but how do I do it? That is a question I am not going to answer, but it is one that, I believe, every clinician here needs to solve.

Let us say that you have managed to solve this problem and spoken about envy, or greed, or jealousy in such a way that there is no hint of condemnation present. What happens? The condemning god is not then installed in the analyst but is experienced, usually as a voice, within. Hidden schizophrenia becomes manifest. It is a very healthy moment when the patient says: "But, my god, this is mad . . ." and realizes how this has thwarted her efforts at becoming a person.

I want now to go back for a moment to my own misdemeanour. Now, in fact, I did rather well in that exam; but what I want to throw light upon is the extent to which *mimetic learning* is endorsed in our culture, but it is more than just learning. What is encouraged is the production of robots. If we sit back and think to ourselves that this is so in totalitarian regimes like Burma or Iraq but not in democracies like America, Israel, Australia, or Britain, then we are seriously deluded. That solicitor of mine was not the exception but the rule. In fact, he was the exception in that he was dissatisfied with being a robot. He had a knowledge in him that there was a better way of existing in the world. What would we do if there were a sudden mass realization? Our consulting-rooms would have long queues outside them. What would we do? Give five-minute sessions like Lacan? Do group psychoanalysis? At the moment society is able to disown this madness, but how? Oh, yes: look, there are the mad people: in the psychiatric units, visiting psychoanalysts, attending psychiatrists as out-patients. They have their own disorder to attend to plus what society projects into them.

We are not talking of the problem of a few individuals, or even of ten per cent of the population. It is *the malaise* of our culture.

I need now to return to the individual and see what has gone wrong. I think it is clear that my formulation is that it is the *narcissistic constellation* within that thwarts the individual's efforts to become her own person. But how has that *constellation* come about?

In his paper "On Arrogance" (1957), Bion says that the analyst is poking about like an archaeologist and discovering evidence of a primitive catastrophe. What I refer to as the *narcissistic constellation* is the living sign of an early disaster. What is it? What is its nature? Now the answer I am going to give you is extremely frustrating, and you may want to rise up and throw me out of the lecture-hall.

The traumatizing factor for the infant, for the young child, for the latency child, for the adolescent is the narcissism of the parents. You may think that this is a cop-out on my part, that this sort of answer solves nothing. I shall address this objection in a moment, but first I should like to make it clear why this is the case. The fundamental reason is that the presence of narcissism stifles emotional giving. The narcissistic mother's capacity to give to her child emotionally becomes restricted. When you take a case history, when a patient communicates her childhood difficulties, her core complaint is that she was deprived of emotional giving. This is not what she will say. Her laments are numerous, but not one of them is the problem itself. She is poking around, like a child in a sand treasure-box, looking for what is wrong. She names this incident, that incident, this thing that the mother did, that thing that the father did, and so on. But none of these is quite it. There are two reasons why she cannot name it:

1. Emotions are not visible.
    and:
2. A presence is easier to grasp than an absence.

Let us think about these two reasons for a moment. You may say that emotions are visible. When someone is in a state of fear, you see her trembling. But the truth of the matter is that you see the trembling and intuit fear. You see someone kissing and stroking another, and you intuit love. In both cases you may be wrong. Love cannot be seen but is experienced. So the patient is trying to articulate a reality that is not sensed directly and—even worse—not about its presence but its absence.

This is *the* traumatizing agent. I should like to encourage you not to be diverted from this. Even in cases where there have been more obvious shocks like sexual abuse or the death of a parent, it is worth keeping this core issue in mind because the outer event *may* divert the clinician's attention from what is primary to what is secondary. It would be an error for a clinician to ignore one in favour of the other, but both need to be held in mind. I am emphasizing absence of emotional giving because it is so often neglected, but the other components of the *narcissistic constellation* need to be thought about. The hateful expulsion of the unacceptable into the infant is enormously important and has been emphasized recently by some clinicians at the Tavistock Clinic. A mother cannot bear the greed in herself, so she hates any sign of it in her baby or growing child and tortures him for it. This is so common that it goes unnoticed. Yet children galore suffer its effects.

I must ask you to exercise your imagination and apply all the elements of the *narcissistic constellation* and see how they hurt the baby. I will give just one more example, and then I must leave it to you. Where is god located in the narcissistic mother? If god is located in herself, then she is distant from her baby, she's an inflated tyrant, and the baby has lost a friend. If she installs god in her husband, then she will alienate her baby from him. If she installs god in the baby, she will defer to its demands without discrimination. I must now leave this to your imaginations to develop further.

It is very difficult clinically to sort this matter out. It is because two narcissistic people are always merged. So your patient and her mother are merged, and there are two clinical errors, both of which damage the patient. The first is where the psychotherapist believes that what the patient says about her mother is a faithful portrait. The mother was or is as the patient has described. The other is where the clinician refers all that is said about the mother to an inner mother inside the patient. Both these extremes injure your patient. The clinical task here is separation of patient from mother. When this is achieved, the patient sees her mother differently. It is that the individual seen through the spectacles of the *narcissistic constellation* is quite different from the person seen through the eyes of sanity. As components of the *narcissistic constellation* are transformed into useful mental functions, so the outer figure is seen as a composite both of health and of narcissism. This process of transformation is concurrent with those generative acts that fashion a person out of parts and particles. All clinical attention therefore should be upon the *narcissistic constellation*. What the real mother is like can only be known by the patient when her own mental functions are operating properly.

* * *

At the moment our theory posits that narcissism is transmitted by narcissism. Once I had a patient with a severe obsessional compulsive disorder; her mother also had severe obsessional compulsive disorder; her grandmother also had severe obsessional compulsive disorder. She wanted children, but she said to me one day: "I want the rot to stop with me. I don't want to pass it on to my children."

Patients come to us to free themselves from a blight to which they are the unfortunate heirs. This is like a genetic inheritance that passes from generation to generation, and the individual's life task is to free herself from it to the greatest degree possible.

But are there no other factors? There are the "disasters of fate". A mother dies when her child is young; the father was forced to work at a long distance from home, so the children had an almost fatherless upbringing. But there are also the calamities perpetrated through a human agency gone mad or bad. The Holocaust, Hiroshima, the crushing of Tibet, the civil war in Yugoslavia, the slave trade in the last centuries, the massacres in present-day Algeria, and the whole catalogue of human crime has lacerated the human community until it is a wonder that people have survived at all. Whenever these disasters strike, all human energy goes into the task of survival. Psychological care is relegated to second place. Children are rushed to a place of safety, be they with their mothers or without them. Their psychological needs are sacrificed in favour of survival. Huge traumas affecting big populations leave, as a legacy, a huge psychological scarring. When we see the ugly scenes following a massacre on television, what we see is the physical destruction. The psychological damage is far greater and more long-lasting. Wilfred Bion said once that we are still suffering the effects of the Battle of Marathon. I do not think this is an exaggerated statement. It would not surprise me if it takes two or three thousand years to recover from the devastation of the Holocaust. These unthinkable events spawn a narcissism that is of epidemic proportions.

This is why I said about my solicitor, at the beginning, that he is one of the few who attempts to do something about it. He feels a fraud because he has not performed that creative act that turns him from being an agglomerative dummy into a living person. I hope the reasons I have given you for why he feels a fake are understandable. I have wanted also to emphasize that this is a very widespread disease. I believe that the clinician's task is to help the individual patient in his endeavour to become a free human being. I believe that the clinician will do this better if he realizes that his patient is attempting something that others fear to do. This perspective creates a favourable environment for the patient to become genuine and cease to be a fake.

REFERENCES

Arendt, H. (1964). *Eichmann in Jerusalem: A Report on the Banality of Evil*. New York: Viking Press.
Berlin, I., & Hardy, H. (ed.) (1979). *Against the Current: Essays in the History of Ideas*. Oxford: Oxford University Press.
Bion, W. R. (1957). On Arrogance. In: *Second Thoughts*. London: Karnac Books 1993.
Bion, W. R. (1967/1993). Development of schizophrenic thought. In: *Second Thoughts*. London: William Heinemann Medical Books/ Karnac.
Bion, W. R. (1974). *Brazilian Lectures II*. Rio de Janeiro: Imago Editora.
Freud, S. (1895d [1893–1895]), with J. Breuer. Studies on Hysteria. In: *S.E., 2*.
Freud, S. (1907b). Obsessive actions and religious practices. In: *S.E., 9*.
Freud, S. (1912–13). *Totem and Taboo*. In: *S.E., 13*.
Freud, S. (1914c). On narcissism: An introduction. In: *S.E., 14*.
Freud, S. (1915b). Thoughts for the times on war and death. In: *S.E., 14*.
Freud, S. (1915f). A case of paranoia running counter to the psycho-analytic theory of the disease. In: *S.E., 14*.
Freud, S. (1916d). Some character-types met with in psycho-analytic work. In: *S.E., 14*.
Freud, S. (1917e [1915]). Mourning and melancholia. In: *S.E., 14*.
Freud, S. (1919a [1918]). Lines of advance in psycho-analytic therapy. In: *S.E., 17*.
Freud, S. (1920g). *Beyond the Pleasure Principle*. In: *S.E., 18*.
Freud, S. (1921c). *Group Psychology and the Analysis of the Ego*. In: *S.E., 18*.
Freud, S. (1922b). Some neurotic mechanisms in jealousy, paranoia and homosexuality. In: *S.E., 18*.
Freud, S. (1923b). *The Ego and the Id*. In: *S.E., 19*.

Freud, S. (1924c). The economic problem of masochism. In: *S.E., 19*.
Freud, S. (1926d [1925]). *Inhibitions, Symptoms and Anxiety*. In: *S.E., 20*.
Freud, S. (1926e). *The Question of Lay Analysis*. In: *S.E., 20*.
Freud, S. (1927c). *The Future of an Illusion*. In: *S.E., 21*.
Freud, S. (1928b). Dostoevsky and parricide. In: *S.E., 21*.
Freud, S. (1930a). *Civilization and Its Discontents*. In: *S.E., 21*.
Freud, S. (1933a). *New Introductory Lectures on Psycho-Analysis*. In: *S.E., 22*.
Freud, S. (1933b [1932]). *Why War?* In: *S.E., 22*.
Freud, S. (1940a [1938]). *An Outline of Psycho-Analysis*. In: *S.E., 23*.
Freud, S. (1950 [1897]). Extracts from the Fliess papers, Letter 71. In: *S.E., 1*.
Greene, G. (1980). *Ways of Escape*. London/Sydney/Toronto: Bodley Head.
Guillaume, A. (1976). *Islam*. Harmondsworth, Middlesex: Penguin Books.
Holy Bible, The: Revised Standard Version (1962). London. Eyre & Spottiswoode.
Jerusalem Bible, The (1966). London: Darton, Longman and Todd.
Hampson, N. (1971). *The Enlightenment*. Harmondsworth, Middlesex: Pelican Books.
Klein, M. (1957). Envy and gratitude. In *The Writings of Melanie Klein, Vol. III: Envy and Gratitude and Other Works*. London: The Hogarth Press and Institute of Psycho-Analysis.
Lecky, W. E. H. (1913). *History of European Morals*. London/New York/Bombay/Calcutta: Longmans, Green & Co.
Macmurray, J. (1936). *Interpreting the Universe*. London: Faber & Faber, 1952.
Newman, J. H. (1888). *A Grammar of Assent*. London: Longmans, Green & Co.
Russell, B. (1974). *History of Western Philosophy*. London: George Allen & Unwin Ltd.
Scholem, G. (1995). *Major Trends in Jewish Mysticism*. New York: Schocken Books.